Higher-Order Thinking

the Multiple Intelligences Way

Higher-Order Thinking

the Multiple Intelligences Way

DAVID LAZEAR

Crown House Publishing Limited
www.crownhouse.co.uk

Higher-Order Thinking the Multiple Intelligences Way

Grades K–12+

© 2004, 2005 by David Lazear

Editing: Kirsteen E. Anderson
Design and Production: Dan Miedaner
Cover: Tom Fitton

First published in 2004 by:
Zephyr Press
An imprint of Chicago Review Press
814 North Franklin Street
Chicago, IL 60610
800-232-2187
www.zephyrpress.com

Original ISBN: 1-56976-157-4
Original LCCN: 2003010009

UK paperback edition published by:
Crown House Publishing Ltd
Crown Buildings
Bancyfelin
Carmarthen
Wales SA33 5ND, UK
www.crownhouse.co.uk

British Library Cataloguing-in-Publication Data
A catalogue entry for this book is available from the British Library.

ISBN 190442483X

Printed and bound in the UK by Cromwell Press, Trowbridge, Wiltshire

Contents _____

Tables _____

Preface

In high school I had an English literature teacher named Mrs. Callie Milstead. She stubbornly maintained that just being able to remember the information presented in class and in our textbooks did not mean we had really learned it. I could never understand what she meant. If I could recall the information to answer questions on a test, then surely I had mastered it! Nonetheless Mrs. Milstead would constantly pester us to find relationships between the bits and pieces of information we were so skilled at reproducing on call. She would ask us to analyze and understand underlying processes and dynamics of the content she was teaching—the writing process; the process of grammar, syntax, and semantics in literature; the dynamic process of a classical Shakespearian drama; and so forth. Her constant refrain was, "If you can't tell me how what we're studying applies to you in your everyday life, then I don't care if you can answer every question with 100 percent accuracy on a test, you don't understand the material! If you can't apply it, you haven't learned it!" Given this definition of learning, I did very little real learning in my formal educational career.

When I was sitting in Callie Milstead's classes, no one was talking about such things as higher-order thinking, metacognition, understanding and developing skillful patterns of thinking, graphic organizers, or cognitive maps. But Callie Milstead was doing it nonetheless. And we learned! We learned how to apply what we were studying. We learned how to transfer insights from English literature to other areas of the curriculum. We learned how to integrate what we were studying into our lives to such an extent that a great deal of it is still with me today.

Callie Milstead was also a master at employing multiple intelligences, although again, that terminology did not yet exist. Howard Gardner had not yet coined the phrase "multiple intelligences" to describe the many different ways we remember what we know, process information, acquire knowledge, learn, and understand. Nevertheless, Mrs. Milstead's classes were multimodal to the hilt! We could never second-guess her. When we entered her classroom we never knew what to expect, other than that whatever we did would delight us, and would be interesting and challenging. We knew our minds would be stretched during that class hour, and that our lives would be touched in ways that would affect us many years into the future.

In some ways, the way Callie Milstead taught is the epitome of what effective teaching has always been. Good teachers have always known that to reach all students, *everything* has to be presented in a wide variety of ways. Good teachers have always known that the proof of the learning comes "when the rubber hits the road," so to speak, not in reproducing answers on some out-of-context test.

Today we have an immense body of research about the human thinking and learning processes and how to improve them; in fact, we know more about what is effective for teaching and learning than humans have ever known. Our increasingly complex world is also urgently requiring that we be multimodal creatures who think at higher-order levels. Given the state-of-the-art research behind our profession, there is no reason to spend time on anything but lessons and units that challenge students to think at higher-order levels and that genuinely prepare them to assume leadership roles in the future.

I dedicate this book to all the Callie Milsteads of our world—past, present, and future. They are the teachers who always have, are still, and always will ensure that "no child is left behind," not only in school but in their lives beyond the walls of formal education!

David G. Lazear
Maui, Hawai'i
Spring 2003

1

Moving Students' Intelligences to Higher-Order Realms

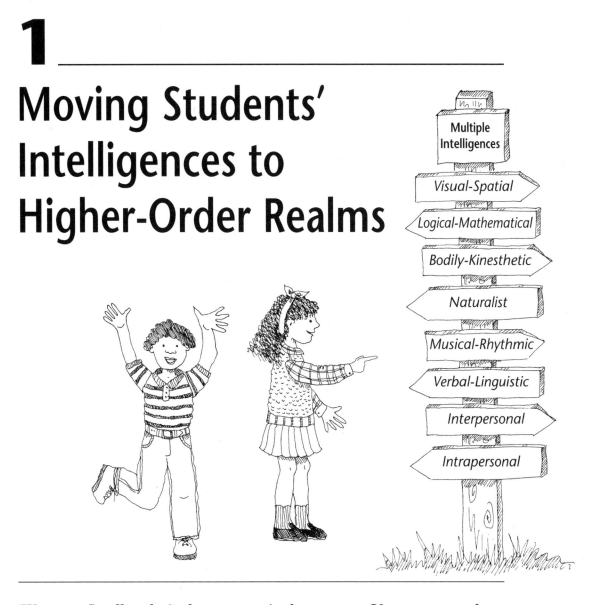

We must finally admit that process is the content. If we want students to develop certain behavioral characteristics—taking a critical stance with their work, inquiring, thinking flexibly, learning from another person's perspective—then we should start with those attributes and focus the entire curriculum on achieving them . . . The core of our curriculum must focus on such processes as learning to learn, knowledge production, metacognition, transference, decision-making, creativity, and group problem solving. These are the subject matters of instruction.
—Art Costa, *Developing Minds*

A group of middle school students are involved in a unit on the process of photosynthesis, learning about the parts of a plant, how they function, and the role each part plays in the larger photosynthesis process. In expert groups, they have used colored markers to create large posters that illustrate each part of the plant and its role in the life of the plant. One group has drawn a cross section of a plant's leaf system, another group has illustrated the workings of the root system, another the plant's reproductive system, and so on, with the functions of each system appropriately labeled. The teams are now sharing their posters with the whole class, explaining the inner workings of their respective part of the plant. The posters are colorful, imaginative, visually appealing, and instructive.

The teacher asks the teams to post their drawings at the front of the class. He explains, "We now have some drawings that represent the basic functions of the parts of a plant. Now we are going to put them together and understand the relationships and dynamics between these parts." He proceeds to give a mini-lecture (based on information from the science textbook) explaining what goes on at each stage of the photosynthesis process:

> *Step one of the process: The rays of the sun strike the plant. This causes the chlorophyll in the plant to turn toward the sun. The chlorophyll grabs the sun's energy and uses it to split the water molecules inside the leaf.*

He then asks the class to think of fun and creative images, patterns, designs, symbols, and pictures they could add to the leaf system poster to show the chlorophyll turning toward the sun to capture its energy. As the students have ideas, they come to the front of the class and draw them on the poster. One student draws little green solar panels on the surface of a leaf. Coming out of the solar panels are funny hands that are grabbing the rays of the sun. Another draws green satellite disks turning toward the sun.

As the instruction continues (using the process of mini-lecture followed by a pause to illustrate each concept), some students begin to draw symbolic connections between the plant's various systems, such as a complex of pipes running from the root system to the leaf system or tiny water trucks traveling along the plant's stem to deliver the water to the leaves. Students have fun finding unusual ways to illustrate the various steps of photosynthesis, and the pictures, shapes, images, designs, and patterns they draw on the posters demonstrate a great deal of understanding of how the different parts of the plant interact during the photosynthesis process.

In the final stage of the lesson, each student receives an 11" x 17" sheet of white construction paper. The class is instructed to imagine they are abstract artists creating a painting for the Museum of Modern Art, entitled *The Process of Photosynthesis*. Using colored markers only, they are to create something that illustrates the process. No words are permitted on their creations! They must tell the story through shapes, images, patterns, colors, designs, and visual symbols.

What you have just read is an example of using multiple intelligences (in this case visual-spatial intelligence) to facilitate higher-order thinking and reasoning in students. As with any higher-order thinking task, the key is to move students from thinking about "the facts, ma'am, nothing but the facts," to understanding the dynamic relationships among the facts and the various processes involved, then to the level of synthesizing, integrating, applying, and transferring the learning. It is at the last level that learning is internalized, is invested with meaning, and becomes part of one's being.

What I have just described is a much simplified version of Benjamin Bloom's now-famous taxonomy of cognitive abilities (Bloom 1956). In my opinion, Bloom's taxonomy is still the best model we have for what is involved in logical-mathematical thought. However, I propose (1) that each of the eight intelligences possesses a unique taxonomy of cognitive abilities, and (2) that educators need to use all the intelligences at their respective higher-order levels in order to promote a deep level of learning and mastery of the curriculum in their students.

When teachers first adopt a multiple intelligences approach to teaching, many use the intelligences either simply to spice up otherwise dry lessons or as mnemonic devices to help students remember certain facts and figures. Of course, the entertainment value of a lesson will certainly be higher when teachers use multiple intelligences in teaching and learning, and this approach will most certainly aid students in remembering the information. From the perspective of the full range of cognitive abilities each intelligence represents, however, such a use of multiple intelligences is akin to never moving beyond the information recall levels of Bloom's taxonomy. In contrast, a deep understanding of the multiple taxonomies of multiple intelligences provides a way to help students think at higher levels in and through the different intelligence domains.

The Cognitive Domains of the Eight Intelligences

Each of the eight intelligences has its own language, its own jargon and vernacular, and its own modus operandi (Lazear 1998b). In *Frames of Mind* (1983), the book in which he presented his original research on the theory of multiple intelligences, Howard Gardner discusses the criteria he used to identify the various intelligences. One criterion was that the intelligence had to have its own symbolic notation system or means of encoding in a symbol system.

> Much of human representation and communication of knowledge takes place via symbol systems—culturally contrived systems of meaning which capture important forms of information. Language, picturing, mathematics are but three of the symbol systems that have become important the world over for human survival and human productivity . . . While it may be possible for an intelligence to proceed without its own special symbol system, or without some other culturally devised arena, a primary characteristic of human intelligence may well be its "natural" gravitation toward embodiment in a symbolic system. (Gardner 1983, 66)

The key to working deeply and effectively with multiple intelligences is immersing yourself in the language system and capacities of the different intelligences. A good analogy for this is experiencing a foreign culture: You will have a much greater understanding of and appreciation for that culture if you speak its language. The same is true for the intelligences, especially with regard to their higher-order cognitive abilities and processes. So, for example, with musical-rhythmic intelligence you are working primarily with knowledge and understanding that is acquired through sound and vibration, including tones, pitch, timbre, beats, rhythms, percussion, music, and all manner of auditory stimuli from the environment, from the human vocal cords, and from machines. With bodily-kinesthetic intelligence you are in a cognitive realm that learns and understands primarily in and through physical movement, such as dance, dramatic enactment, role play, mime, facial expressions, postures, physical games, or body language. You must learn to speak the language and operate within the cognitive domains of the different intelligences in order to understand the information you receive.

Part of the difficulty of working with multiple intelligences from an instructional-assessment point of view is that only verbal-linguistic intelligence uses a verbal language system. The remaining intelligences use ways of knowing other than the spoken, written, or read word.

Visual-spatial intelligence uses the language of shapes, images, patterns, designs, color, textures, pictures, visual symbols, and "inner seeing" (such things as active imagination, pretending, and visualization).

Bodily-kinesthetic intelligence uses the language of physical movement and thus involves such things as creative and interpretive dance, drama, mime, role play, gesture, body language, facial expressions, posture, physical games, and physical exercise.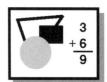

Logical-mathematical intelligence uses the language of recurring patterns (involving numbers, words, geometric designs, and others), problem-solving tactics, and strategizing to meet new challenges.

Naturalist intelligence uses the language of natural patterns, flora, fauna, species groupings, subspecies categorizations, external and internal sensory experiences of the natural world, and all manner of encounters with plants, animals, water, and weather, ranging from microscopic, inorganic matter to natural phenomena seen with the naked eye.

Musical-rhythmic intelligence (which I have begun calling the **auditory-vibrational intelligence**) uses the language of tones, resonance, beats, vibrational patterns, timbre, pitch, rhythms, and all types of sounds (including sounds from the environment, human-produced sounds, sounds from machines, and sounds from musical and percussion instruments).

Verbal-linguistic intelligence uses the language of the spoken word (including formal and informal speech), reading others' writing, writing oneself (including poetry, essays, persuasive writing, and so on), storytelling, and linguistically based humor (such as riddles, jokes, puns, limericks, and plays on words).

Interpersonal intelligence uses the language of human relationships, collaboration, teamwork, cooperation, distinctions among people, common goals, consensus, empathy, and meaningful encounters with others.

Intrapersonal intelligence uses the language of introspection and awareness of internal aspects of the self, including awareness of one's own feelings, intuitions, thought processes, "who am I?" quests, spiritual pursuits, beliefs, and values.

Another qualifying criterion for an intelligence in Gardner's original research was a clearly identifiable set of core operations within the brain, mind, and body system that are stimulated by input from the external world:

> Central to my notion of an intelligence is the existence of one or more basic information-processing operations or mechanisms, which can deal with specific kinds of input. One might go so far as to define a human intelligence as a neural mechanism or computational system which is genetically programmed to be activated or "triggered" by certain kinds of internally or externally presented information. (Gardner 1983, 64)

In other words, these core operations, once triggered in the brain-mind-body system, are able to process, interpret, and understand those certain kinds of information peculiar to each different way of knowing. For example, in the case of verbal-linguistic intelligence, information presented via the written or spoken word would be meaningless if it did not stimulate the language centers of the brain (primarily Broca's area, which is the main language production center of the brain, Wernicke's area for language comprehension, and the temporal lobes where language memory is held). In the case of visual-spatial intelligence, we could conceivably receive much visual stimulation, but it would be confusing and perceived as irrelevant if it did not stimulate the parietal and occipital lobes in the right hemisphere of the brain. (The parietal lobes perceive shapes, images, colors, textures, and patterns, whereas the occipital lobes interpret and make sense of those shapes, images, colors, textures, and patterns.)

In my work, I have referred to these core operations as intelligence capacities. I have also suggested that development of these capacities is the key to strengthening all the intelligences. The better students are in using the different capacities, the easier it is for them to move to the higher-order realms of that intelligence. Table 1 (pages 8–9) summarizes these capacities for each intelligence. For more detailed descriptions, please refer to my books *Eight Ways of Knowing* (1998) and *The Intelligent Curriculum* (2000). In *Eight Ways of Knowing* you will also find a series of exercises that can help you learn how to access and develop each of the intelligences in your own and your students' lives.

Once we move inside an intelligence and its capacities, we are suddenly confronted with a staggering array of cognitive abilities unique to that intelligence. For example, interpersonal intelligence involves much more than just working with other people. It involves such abilities as empathizing; building consensus in a group; appreciating and respecting opinions, beliefs, values, and perspectives that differ from one's own; mastering the complex set of social skills needed to be an effective member of a team; knowing how to deal with disagreement and conflict in a group; understanding processes for group problem solving; setting realistic goals; evaluating the dynamics of a group; and knowing how to help a group alter its dynamics when necessary. Consider bodily-kinesthetic intelligence. It is much, much more than the ability to perform various kinds of movements. It also includes the infant's potential to walk, the ability to develop and train both gross and fine motor skills at almost any stage of development, and the subtleties of expressing oneself through facial expressions, posture, and other body language. And we must not forget muscular imagination, through which we possess the ability, via active mental performance, to improve, strengthen, and refine the movements and functioning of the physical body.

The premise of this book is that in order to work meaningfully with an intelligence, we must understand and be able to use its unique patterns of thinking. Once we have some understanding of the unique way each intelligence thinks, perceives, and understands the world, we can help students access the full cognitive potentials of the eight intelligences in order to master the required curriculum. To accomplish this, we utilize what I am calling the multiple taxonomies of multiple intelligences; namely, the complex of cognitive skills and abilities specific to each intelligence.

Taxonomies of the Eight Intelligences

In the following chapters, I illustrate how to work with the different intelligences at basic, complex, and higher-order cognitive realms. These categories are based on Gardner's discussion of an intelligence's developmental trajectory, or its distinct developmental history (Gardner 1983, 1987). Although the developmental journey is specific to each intelligence, the underlying template applies across all the intelligences. Generally, the development of an intelligence begins at the *basic*, or novice, level, the raw patterning of the intelligence, which usually occurs in early childhood. Development progresses to the *complex* level, which involves a more disciplined acquisition of the skills and abilities of that intelligence. The *higher-order* level involves the integration and synthesis of the intelligence into one's regular repertoire for living. The mastery of an intelligence domain usually manifests through the application of that intelligence in one's vocational or avocational pursuits (also sometimes referred to as "intelligence end states"; Gardner 1999).

Table 1: Understanding the Core Capacities of the Multiple Intelligences

Visual-Spatial Intelligence	Logical-Mathematical Intelligence	Bodily-Kinesthetic Intelligence	Naturalist Intelligence
Mental Images: Creating mental pictures of things perceived in the real world or an imagined external world	**Inductive Reasoning:** Thinking from parts to wholes or from specific examples to generalizations	**Control of Voluntary Movements:** Making the body consciously respond to what the mind wants it to do	**Communion with Nature:** Recognizing patterns of connection between oneself and the larger patterns of the natural world
Graphic Representation: Creating visual illustrations of concepts, processes, ideas, and emotions	**Deductive Reasoning:** Thinking from wholes and generalities to parts and specifics	**Control of Preprogrammed Movements:** Controlling actions that require little thought or conscious intention	**Ability to Live Off the Land:** Nurturing a special relationship with the earth through tilling the soil
Active Imagination: Forming visual connections that transform apparent chaos into creative images	**Complex Calculations:** Understanding relationships in numerical, mathematical, and logical patterns	**Mind-Body Connection:** Altering one's physical being through content in the mind	**Sensitivity to Flora and Fauna:** Appreciating and understanding the plant kingdom
Recognition of Relationships among Objects: Seeing connections between different objects	**Scientific Reasoning:** Solving problems via empirical observation, weighing data, analysis, and evaluation	**Awareness throughout the Body:** Listening to and trusting the feedback received throughout the body	**Ability to Care for, Tame, and Interact with Living Creatures:** Appreciating and understanding the animal kingdom
Orientation in Space: Understanding spatial information and getting around different geographical locations	**Recognition of Relationships and Connections:** Making sense of the complex data that bombard one daily	**Mimetic Abilities:** Learning by observing others and imitating their actions, or by role playing and acting things out	**Appreciation of Nature's Impact:** Attuning oneself to the full sensory impact of the natural world
Accurate Perception from Different Angles: Recognizing similarities and differences between objects from different vantage points	**Abstract Pattern Recognition:** Discerning myriad types of patterns in the surrounding environment	**Improved Body Functioning:** Re-educating the central nervous system through movement mindfulness	**Recognition and Classification of Species:** Seeing and understanding categories of flora and fauna based on distinguishing characteristics
Mental Manipulation of Images: Creating visual illusions such as perspective or 3-D images and being able to shift perspective			

Higher-Order Thinking, © 2004 Zephyr Press, Chicago, IL • 800-232-2187 • www.zephyrpress.com

Table 1: Understanding the Core Capacities of the Multiple Intelligences

Musical-Rhythmic Intelligence	Verbal-Linguistic Intelligence	Interpersonal Intelligence	Intrapersonal Intelligence

Sensitivity to Sound: Processing the wide range of auditory stimuli (tones, beats, vibrational patterns, and so on) that influence daily life **Appreciation for the Structure of Music/Rhythm:** Understanding the evocative power of music, rhythm, sound, and vibration **Awareness of Characteristic Qualities of Tone:** Using various tonal qualities to enhance and deepen communication of ideas, thoughts, emotion, and concepts **Recognition, Creation, and Reproduction of Music, Tones, or Sound:** Repeating or mimicking a rhythmic or tonal pattern **Formation of Schemas and Frames for Hearing Music:** Making conscious (or unconscious) associations and connections between a variety of sounds, music, rhythms, and beats	**Understanding the Order and Meaning of Words:** Grasping word meanings in context and shifting meaning and context by rearranging words **Metalinguistic Analysis:** Using language to investigate and comprehend language **Explanation, Teaching, and Learning:** Giving accurate verbal or written instructions to others and being able to follow such directions **Appreciation of Linguistically Based Humor:** Understanding plays on words, twists of meaning, and the contexts in which language is humorous **Verbal Memory and Recall:** Accessing or retrieving verbal information from short- and long-term memory **Persuasion:** Using the spoken and written word to influence and motivate others **Expressive and Creative Writing:** Communicating feelings, new ideas, fantasy, or settings through written language	**Effective Verbal and Nonverbal Communication:** Understanding and skillfully using words and nonverbal information to enhance communication **Recognition of Moods, Temperaments, and Feelings:** Using subtle feedback from others to guide how one works with them and helps them **Cooperative Work in a Group:** Learning to do one's part and support others in a team effort **Deep Listening to and Understanding of Others:** Focusing fully on a person's communication, shutting off one's own mind chatter **Empathy:** understanding others' perspectives and experiences **Synergy:** Creating and maintaining a spontaneous cooperation in which the final product of a group effort is more than the sum of individual contributions	**Mental Concentration:** Bringing the mind to a point of focus and holding it there **Mindfulness:** Being aware of life's details and the moment-by-moment process of being **Emotional Processing:** Thinking about, understanding, and improving one's own affective (feelings, emotions, and moods) processes **Higher-Order Thinking and Reasoning:** Moving from facts and data to understanding processes, then to application and integration in one's own life **Transpersonal Sense of Self:** Awareness of oneself as part of the network of humanity, the universe, and the cosmos **Awareness and Expression of Feelings:** Being in touch with, understanding, and using the emotional or affective domain

In this book I have transformed the developmental journey for each intelligence into a taxonomy of cognitive abilities. Each chapter presents a table describing the thought processes inherent to the different intelligence domains at different levels of thinking based on a simplified version of Bloom's taxonomy. The basic template I used to analyze the taxonomies of the multiple intelligences appears in table 2.

Gathering and Understanding Basic Knowledge

This level is primarily concerned with learning and comprehending the basic facts, figures, definitions, components, distinct pieces of information, and concepts related to a specific topic. This is the level where learning begins; but, unfortunately, in formal education this is also often where it ends.

"Just give me the facts ma'am, nothing but the facts!"

There is a mistaken assumption that someone who has simply memorized these basic facts, figures, definitions, components, distinct pieces of information, and concepts, and can reproduce them in an acceptable form on demand, has been educated! This is obviously a bit of an overstatement; yet, when you consider the weight given to standardized test scores in our society—tests that to a greater or lesser degree are testing students' ability to remember knowledge they have gathered—it is not as much of an overstatement as I would wish.

Gathering and understanding knowledge generally involves such things as
- mastering the terminology and core concepts of the content involved in the unit
- memorizing the key facts, figures, data, and so on that will be used during the unit
- learning how to perform certain processes or operations at the heart of the content
- understanding certain classifications or groupings of information
- summarizing or explaining concepts to others

Processing and Analyzing Information

After having acquired the basic information about a topic, one can then start to put the pieces of information together, so to speak. This is the level of thinking where students are asked to think about and discover how the distinct pieces of information they have gathered relate to each other. They learn about the dynamic nature of the information. They analyze which parts are dependent on other parts and which parts seem to be relatively independent.

"How does it work? When should I use it?"

Table 2. Application of Bloom's Taxonomy to the Multiple Intelligences

Level of Thought	Aspects and Activities of the Level	Thought Processes to Stimulate the Level
Higher-Order Thinking & Reasoning **3**	**Synthesizing** • using the knowledge to produce a novel communication • designing plans for using, implementing, or applying the knowledge • grasping abstract relations and connections to other pieces of knowledge **Evaluating** • examining internal evidence and consistency of the learned information • examining external evidence and consistency of the learned information • investing learning with personal meaning and significance	design, redesign, combine, add to, compose, hypothesize, construct, imagine, draw if . . . then conclusions, integrate with other learning, create, apply interpret, judge, criticize, decide, estimate, forecast, speculate, explain the significance of, tell personal meanings
Processing & Analyzing Information **2**	**Processing** • using information learned in specific, concrete situations • understanding the dynamics or procedures inherent in the information • grasping the significance of the information and when to use it **Analyzing** • breaking down learned information into its key elements • analyzing relationships among key elements • analyzing the organizational principles of the information	apply, solve, experiment, distinguish, sort, infer, explain why, deduce, compare and contrast connect, relate, differentiate, classify, arrange, group, interpret, organize, categorize, take apart, analyze
Gathering & Understanding Basic Knowledge **1**	**Gathering** • learning specific facts, figures, and pieces of knowledge • learning to manipulate or deal with pieces of knowledge • learning structures and theories underlying the knowledge **Understanding** • paraphrasing or translating the knowledge gathered • explaining the information to someone else • extrapolating from specific pieces of information	define, recognize, recall, identify, label, understand, examine, categorize, show, collect, generalize, sequence, classify, match, count translate, say it in your own words, explain to someone else, describe, summarize, demonstrate

They learn how to connect the new learning to previous knowledge and to learning that may have occurred in totally different content areas. And they begin the process of figuring out when and how the new information might be useful.

Processing and analyzing information generally involves such things as
- asking questions about the gathered information, such as, Where did this come from? or How was it discovered?
- breaking the information into its composite parts and learning how each part contributes to the whole
- learning why and how certain processes, operations, concepts, and so forth are important to the content area being studied; for example, what if there had been no Boston Tea Party?
- comparing and contrasting different parts of the information
- examining how other people make use of the information outside a formal educational setting
- exploring relationships between this information and other areas of the school curriculum

Higher-Order Thinking and Reasoning

Some thinking-skills researchers suggest that this level is the ultimate assessment of what learning has occurred in a lesson or unit; namely, Do students know what to do with information beyond the formal, academic situation? Can they apply it? Do they see connections between what they have supposedly learned and previous knowledge? Are they able to invest the acquired knowledge with personal meaning and significance so that it becomes a part of their repertoire for living? Can they use this knowledge or information to create knowledge and information? I would propose that this level is where we empower students to be effective, productive contributors to our society. This is the level where students acquire values and learn responsibility for creating the future.

"So, what's it good for, anyway? How am I going use it?"

Synthesizing and evaluating (the heart of higher-order thinking) generally involves such things as
- exploring personal implications of the information learned: How will this make a difference in my life?
- articulating changes in perspective: How has this changed my understanding of myself and my world?
- making personal judgments about the relative importance of the information to oneself
- making plans for how to use the information in daily life
- integrating the information with other knowledge or information

Applying the Taxonomies

Part of any unit of instruction (often several days' worth!) will be spent at the gathering and understanding level. Here students use the intelligences to gather and understand basic concepts; for example, you might have them draw pictures of the concepts being studied, or act them out, or make up songs, raps, or jingles to aid basic recall. As the unit progresses, however, and students have represented the key facts, figures, definitions, and so on using several intelligences, you can then move them to the level of analyzing and processing the information. In the example that opens this chapter, students are engaged in seeing, visualizing, and drawing the connections and dynamic relationships in the drawings they created at the gathering and understanding level. Yet, as interesting and creative as the processing and analyzing level may be, the more time you can spend in higher-order thinking and reasoning, and the more involved and complex you can make the learning tasks at this level, the more you can promote transfer, application, synthesis, and integration of the concepts involved in the unit. In the final level, the concepts move from what is often called book learning or classroom learning to life learning; that is, students are learning about themselves and their lives in the world beyond school.

The unique taxonomies presented in each chapter must be *spiraled* in accordance with developmentally appropriate practices for students at different ages (see Bruner 1966), but the cognitive cues presented for the different levels in the taxonomy tables apply regardless of age. Each chapter also illustrates ways to apply selected taxonomies to specific units of instruction at the elementary, middle, and high school levels. In the appendix is a worksheet to help you design your own units that access higher-order realms of the different intelligences.

Earlier I mentioned that working with the taxonomies for multiple intelligences makes lessons more interesting and definitely aids students in remembering information. But the benefits go far beyond this. When students are provided the opportunity to understand their own many intelligences, or ways of knowing, and are given frequent opportunities to use them in lessons, not only are they more actively involved with the material at hand, but they also make many more personal connections with what they are studying, thus investing it with meaning. Teaching students about the different intelligences and how to use them gives them many tools for greater success in school, as well as for success in life beyond the classroom.

2

The Object-Related Forms of Intelligence

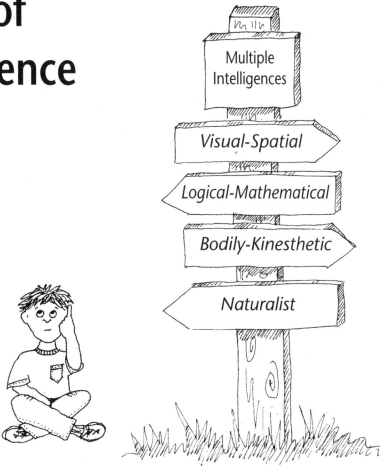

The "object-related" forms of intelligences . . . are subject to one kind of control: that actually exerted by the structure and the functions of the particular objects with which individuals come into contact. Were our physical universe structured differently, these intelligences would presumably assume different forms.

—Howard Gardner, *Frames of Mind*

In his early research, Howard Gardner (e.g., 1983) listed **visual-spatial, logical-mathematical, and bodily-kinesthetic** intelligences in this category. In my work I have added the **naturalist** intelligence to this group.

The object-related intelligences have in common modes of cognition that rely on objects that either exist in the real world or can be imagined. Examples of such objects are concrete shapes, patterns, colors, images, designs, and other things that we come in contact with or interact with on a daily basis. Among them are not only objects created by humans—such as buildings, machines, art, or technological inventions—but also the full range of objects, shapes, patterns, and colors existing in the natural world. Imagined objects, those we see in our mind's eye, are also tapped by these intelligences. Gardner (1983) suggests it is the very existence of these things that "triggers" the object-related intelligences. In other words, without objects to interact with, these intelligences would have nothing to do!

Thus, in lessons or units that use any of the object-related intelligences in order to move up the taxonomy of cognitive abilities, you would work directly with the concrete media of the relevant intelligence. It is the encounters with these media that stimulate this group of intelligences. In the following pages I present background information on each object-related intelligence, followed by a sampling of the range of cognitive tools, strategies, techniques, and methodologies that access each "way of knowing." In table form I present a taxonomy that illustrates how you might employ the tools and strategies of a given intelligence to promote higher-order thinking and reasoning in your classroom.

Visual-Spatial Intelligence Taxonomy
A Picture Is Worth a Thousand Words

Perhaps the most extraordinary and distinctive ability humans possess is imagination. We can see, hear, and feel people, places, and future possibilities using inner eyes, ears, and other senses. They allow us to soar across landscapes of our own creation. Imagination often leads to the Aha! experience in discovery. It forms the basis of "in-sight," whether in art, science or our personal lives.
—Terry Marks-Tarlow, *Creativity Inside Out: Learning through Multiple Intelligences*

The visual-spatial way of knowing is one of the earliest acquired in human development. Before we develop language to talk about the various objects, colors, shapes, and places that make up the external world of our daily lives, we form pictures of these things in our minds. We could say that visual-spatial intelligence is our first language. The brain naturally thinks in images and pictures even before it has words to attach to them. We could no more stop our brains from forming mental images than we could our lungs from taking in oxygen! Infants quickly learn to recognize the faces of important people in their lives, their bottles, and their favorite toys because they have mental representations of these objects as well as imaged associations and experiences with them. Ancient peoples of almost every culture used these types of images to communicate through varieties of hieroglyphs, petroglyphs, and cave paintings.

In your mind's eye can you see the place where you grew up? Can you picture where your car is parked? Can you see the faces of your children, your spouse, or someone special to you? These are examples of visual-spatial knowing. Allow me to share two personal examples of the power of this way of knowing.

My youngest daughter, Naomi, is very strong in this intelligence. In school she drove her teachers crazy by endlessly doodling during lectures. Every margin of every worksheet or paper was filled with little pictures, images, squiggles, doodles, and so on. She carried a secret supply of colored markers in her purse. When the teacher's back was turned, out came the markers and she would add color to her drawings. Teacher after teacher would admonish her, "Naomi, put those markers away and pay attention!" She would put the markers away, but as soon as the markers were put away, she no longer paid attention. Something about those doodles, pictures, images, and squiggles kept her involved in the lesson or what was happening in the classroom.

Fortunately, when she reached junior high school, Naomi met a teacher who had learned the skill of Mind Mapping (see the Mind Mapping exercise on page 20). Mind Mapping is a process invented by Tony Buzan (see, for example, *Use Both Sides of Your Brain*). A Mind Map is basically a pictorial representation of specific information. This teacher taught Naomi how to channel her seemingly aimless doodling into a note-taking technique. This tool was so powerful for her that once she had created a Mind Map during a lecture, she did not need to refer to it again. When she wanted to recall the information, for example during a test, she would simply close her eyes, retrieve the Mind Map she had created in her mind's eye, and all the information would be there before her. It was almost as if she went to a box of slide photos, pulled out the appropriate one, and projected it on a screen!

The second example comes from Hawai'i, where I live about eight months of the year. I am in awe of the visual-spatial capacities of the ancient Polynesians and other peoples who journeyed to and eventually inhabited the islands of the South Pacific. They traveled thousands of miles across the open ocean, with no sophisticated navigational equipment, no maps, and no compasses. How on earth did they find their way? We don't know exactly, but we know they used at least two methods. One was careful observation and understanding of the ocean wave patterns, which to the knowledgeable communicate exactly where one is in the ocean. The people of the Marshall Islands created stick maps, based on the ocean wave patterns, that told them where other islands were not only in their island chain, but across the entire South Pacific. The second method of navigation was careful observation of the flights of birds. Another example of Hawaiians' spatial sense is seen in the way they give directions based on where you are in relation to the ocean and the mountains; for example, *makai* means toward the ocean and *mauka* means toward the mountains, or away from the ocean.

Overview of the Visual-Spatial Taxonomy of Cognitive Abilities

As I mentioned in chapter 1, the unique language of visual-spatial intelligence is coded in shapes, images, patterns, designs, colors, textures, shapes, and pictures that we can observe either with our physical eyes or with our mind's eye. Thus, working with the taxonomy of cognitive abilities for this intelligence will involve knowing, analyzing, and processing information through images and pictures, shapes, colors, textures, and patterns. In practice this means using a full range of visual media—including colored markers, construction paper, paints, and fabric—working with clay and other sculpting media; and using photography and video recording. It also encompasses a number of "inner seeing" abilities, including such things as visualizing, pretending, imagining, forming mental images, and various guided imagery processes.

Here are professions and activities that draw heavily on visual-spatial intelligence. According to Gardner (1983), it is often in vocational pursuits that we see the ultimate development and potential of the intelligences:

cartographers   *theater set designers*
interior decorators   *professional drivers*
chefs (food presentation)   *cinematographers*
architects   *illustrators*
quilters/needlepointers   *painters/sculptors*
airline pilots   *tour guides*
landscapers   *jewelry/clothing designers*
photographers   *drafters*

Visual-Spatial Abilities
The following are the key cognitive abilities
of visual-spatial intelligence

Visual Illustrating: Creating representations of one's learning and understanding using the media of the visual arts. One example is collecting a series of pictures or objects to create a montage or collage that shows various aspects or dimensions of a concept, idea, or process. Students could also use colored paints or markers to make a mural that expresses their learning. They could also create presentation slides on a computer using such programs as Power Point or Key Note.

Mental Imagery: Using various processes of seeing with the mind's eye to extend learning. These are activities in the realms of the active imagination, pretend, and fantasy. Students learn to use the processes of visualization and guided imagery to create images of different concepts in their minds (such as characters in a story, a period of history, a scientific process).

Sculpting and Building: Applying the same basic processes described in visual illustrating but using different media: clay, papier-mâché, building materials, tinfoil, or anything else that can be shaped. These activities tap a different set of cognitive abilities often associated with architects, inventors, or sculptors.

Flow Charts and Graphing: Visually showing the dynamic relationships among concepts being studied using bar graphs, flow charts, pie charts, and the like. Another specialized example is a Mind Map (see p. 20). Through these various kinds of charts and graphs, students learn to recognize and represent interrelationships between concepts.

Photography and Video Recording: Tapping visual technology to help students visually represent things they are learning. Such activities involve working with camcorders, creating movies on a computer, taking pictures with a digital camera, or using digital photo enhancement/alteration software (such as Photoshop) to create a photographic montage or video documentary related to material being taught and learned.

The Basic Mind Mapping Process

Following are suggestions to help you create your own Mind Maps.

1. Start in the center of the page by writing the topic and a symbolic representation of it.

2. Draw branches out from the central image for each association you have with the central topic, creating patterns, symbols, colors, and images that reflect the associations.

3. Use key words and phrases to help you remember the associations you have represented in your drawings.

4. Use color and three-dimensional perspective in your symbols.

5. Print, rather than write, any words for more distinct and memorable images.

6. Put the words on the branches, not at the ends of them, and use only one word or short phrase per branch.

7. Make the patterns, colors, and images noteworthy, even odd. The mind will remember them better.

8. Use arrows, colors, designs, and so on to show connections among parts of the Mind Map.

9. Build the Mind Map quickly. The more spontaneous it is, the better you capture associations as they occur to you.

10. Be creative and original.

11. Have fun.

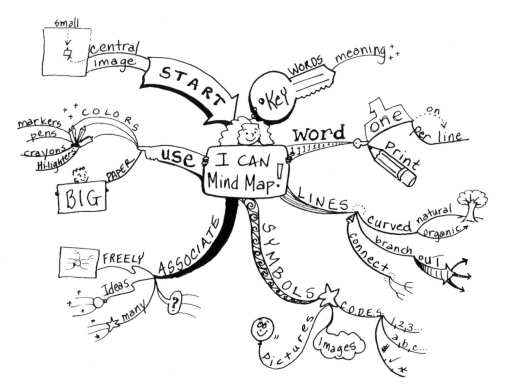

From *Mapping Inner Space: Learning and Teaching Visual Mapping* by Nancy Margulies with Nusa Maal
© 2002, 2004 Zephyr Press, Chicago, IL

Visual-Spatial Cognitive Taxonomy

The following illustrates general visual-spatial applications at each level of the cognitive taxonomy. Table 3 (page 22) illustrates how the previously described visual-spatial abilities could be applied to learning activities at each level of the hierarchy.

3

Higher-Order Thinking & Reasoning
Applying one's learning, reflections, and insights to the creation of abstract, symbolic representations using both external and internal imagery

↑

2

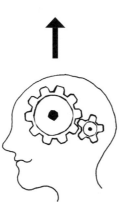

Information Analysis & Processing
Using the skills of visual representation and inner imagery to represent relationships, dynamics, and processes of learning

↑

1

Gathering & Understanding Basic Knowledge
Reproducing objects, colors, shapes, textures, pictures, patterns, and images observed in the external world to assist in remembering information

Table 3: Applying the Cognitive Taxonomy to Visual-Spatial Intelligence

Taxonomy of Cognitive Levels	Visual-Spatial Abilities				
	Visual Illustrating	Mental Imagery	Sculpting & Building	Flow Charts & Graphing	Photography & Video Recording
3 Higher-Order Thinking & Reasoning	Create impressionistic and expressionistic art works that interpret things encountered in the external world	Use various forms of mental imagery as an integral part of the creative process for understanding and making meaning	Create impressionistic or expressionistic art forms to represent abstract, symbolic, or metaphorical under-standings	Demonstrate and interpret elaborate, nonobvious, linear and nonlinear dynamic relationships among a set of items	Present a compelling and unusual visual interpretation of the material that evokes an emotional response in the viewer
2 Information Analysis & Processing	Use depth, dimension, perspective, and a variety of colors and textures to represent things seen in the external world	Use active imagination and guided imagery to amplify and expand understanding and learning	Construct items that interpret dynamic relationships and processes of things observed in the real world	Demonstrate multiple, linear connections and relationships among a variety of separate items	Tell a story about something seen or experienced in a thoughtful visual composition
1 Gathering Basic Knowledge	Create simple drawings, shapes, patterns, or textures that mimic or reproduce things observed in the external world	Use mental imagery, visualization, and pretending as an aid in memorizing facts and figures	Create sculptures or constructions that more or less duplicate objects in the external world	Show clear, linear (one-to-one) relationships or connections between single independent items	Record interesting sets of individual images seen or experienced using video footage or photographs

Higher-Order Thinking, © 2004 Zephyr Press, Chicago, IL • 800-232-2187 • www.zephyrpress.com

Bodily-Kinesthetic Intelligence Taxonomy
The Way to Learn Is by Doing

The body is more than simply another machine, indistinguishable from the artificial objects of the world. It is also the vessel of the individual's sense of self, his most personal feelings and aspirations, as well as that entity to which others respond in a special way because of their uniquely human qualities.
—Howard Gardner, *Frames of Mind*

In *The Intelligent Curriculum* I commented that of all the intelligences, bodily-kinesthetic intelligence may be the most often taken for granted because in our daily lives we perform a wide variety of very complex physical tasks without giving them a second thought. In workshops I will often illustrate this by asking people to think through every movement, every muscle reflex, every shift of weight, every signal the brain sends, and so on, involved in the "simple" act of standing up from a sitting position. Try it right now! Mentally go through the steps you think are involved, then test yourself by actually standing, paying attention to all the things you overlooked in your mental run-through. Keep practicing until your mental image and the actual process of standing are the same.

As you can see from this exercise, every physical movement involves incredible complexity that we take for granted. When an object is thrown to us, we instinctively catch it or duck to avoid being hit by it. Our body "knows" our telephone number or the layout of a computer keyboard. Have you ever tried to remember your phone number when asked by an operator or when placing a call on a rotary phone? Can you lay out the computer keyboard on a piece of paper without moving your fingers to identify the keys? Finally, just consider how often people accidentally hurt themselves when they pick up a heavy object or they walk on an icy sidewalk simply because they are unaware of (or not paying attention to) how their body works and moves.

Some physical movements are carefully and methodically learned through careful and repeated practice. Reflect on your own experiences. What physical skills have you taught yourself to perform? Can you remember the physical skills you had to acquire to become a driver or to perform your favorite sport? Once you have carefully learned these things, however, many of them become almost unconscious or second nature. An elderly couple I know recently decided to take up bicycling for cardiovascular exercise. They are in their late seventies and have not been on bikes in years. One evening, when I was at their home for dinner, one of them took me aside and said, "David, I must be insane. I've not been on a bicycle in a hundred years. I'm probably going to break my neck!" A couple of months later, after they had been bicycling for several weeks, I asked my friend how it was going. He told me "It's a piece of cake! Once I was back on the bike, it was like I was a kid again. Somehow, I remembered how to do it after all these years!" Once the body learns something, it rarely forgets.

As adults many of our daily movements are automatic, but at one time, they were not so easy. A number of years ago I had to undergo foot surgery. Following the surgery I had to wear a large shoe cast to hold the foot immobile during the healing process. When I no longer needed to wear the shoe, and was permitted to walk normally again, I was shocked to discover the full range of things involved in walking, most of which I had never thought about. Movements I had previously taken for granted I could no longer perform without great attention and awareness. It was almost like having to learn to walk all over again! An injury will often bring the extent of our bodily-kinesthetic learning home to us in a powerful and unforgettable way.

Let me share one more example of the powerful knowing that can happen in and through our bodies. In graduate school I had a friend who was studying to become a professional dancer. For a choreography class, he had to create an original dance for performance. After working for a number of weeks on creating the dance, he asked several friends to be an audience so he could practice the dance for a live group. I was amazed. He proceeded through a set of steps, leaps, spins, and other movements I did not know the human body could perform. At the conclusion of the dance we all applauded, and I remember saying to him, "Jim, that was fantastic! Now, could you tell me what was the meaning of the dance? What were you trying to express through it?" He simply looked at me with disappointment on his face. Then he rewound the tape, started the music, and proceeded to dance the dance again. At the conclusion he said to me, "That is the meaning of the dance! If I could have expressed it in any other way, I would not have needed to create the dance!" There are some things in our lives that can be expressed only in and through the body. They must literally be embodied. Consider, for example, the difference between reading a play and seeing it performed.

Part of working with bodily-kinesthetic intelligence involves training ourselves to be more aware of how our bodies move and function when performing a wide range of so-called automatic movements—complex sets of movements we perform every day without giving them a second thought—such as getting up out of a chair, walking, combing our hair, feeding ourselves, and so on. These things may seem simple, and we usually take them very much for granted. But an extremely complex set of functions occurs in the brain-mind-body system when we perform any physical movement.

Most of us living in the western world are somewhat reserved or, frankly, embarrassed to use the full innate capacities of our physical bodies. When it comes to the body, we'd just rather not discuss it, thank you very much! In the early years of our schooling, a great deal of movement is a regular part of every day. As we move through school, however, we tend to move less and less year by year so that, very often, by the time we reach high school, the only significant movement that happens in our day is when we change periods. The net result of this is a general shutting down of these bodily-kinesthetic capacities. This does not have to be the case, however.

Overview of the Bodily-Kinesthetic Taxonomy of Cognitive Abilities

The unique language of the bodily-kinesthetic intelligence is the language of the body. It involves such things as dance, drama, mime, role play, physical exercise, physical games, walking, facial expressions, body postures, gestures, and anything that moves the body. Work with the cognitive abilities for this intelligence involves knowing, analyzing, and processing information in and through physical movement. The movements involve both gross motor activities—such as running, jumping, climbing, and crawling—and more subtle fine motor skills such as a frown, a flick of the wrist, or a raised eyebrow.

Here are professions and activities that draw heavily on bodily-kinesthetic intelligence. According to Gardner (1983), it is often in vocational pursuits that we see the ultimate development and potential of the intelligences:

actors	*doctors/nurses*
builders	*inventors*
athletes	*choreographers*
dancers	*exercise instructors*
hikers/runners/walkers	*sports coaches*
circus artists	*mechanics*
bodybuilders	*law enforcement officers*
physical therapists	

Bodily-Kinesthetic Abilities
The following are the key cognitive abilities
of bodily-kinesthetic intelligence

Dramatic Enactment: Employing the tools of the actor to explore and learn concepts or to demonstrate knowledge and understanding. Thus, students engage in such things as role plays, mimes, charades, acting things out, and so on. They are literally performing their learning.

Body Language: Using all the expressive possibilities of the body, such as facial expressions, postures, gestures, body proximity, and so on, to enhance and deepen the learning process; for example, using subtle body movements alone to communicate feelings about a current event.

Dance and Movement: Learning in and through physical movement. Students learn to use classical dances and physical games to enhance learning and understanding about the world. They also invent new ones, such as a dance to show the process of chemical bonding.

Skill Performance: Tapping the human capacity to learn a skill and perform it at increasing levels of mastery until it becomes part of one's repertoire for living. In the classroom, students demonstrate understanding of a topic through proficient execution of related activities, skills, and abilities.

Inventing Projects: Using project work to help students more fully grasp the meanings and implications of what they are studying. They create an experiential or hands-on demonstration that helps others learn about the topic by doing it.

Bodily-Kinesthetic Cognitive Taxonomy

The following illustrates general bodily-kinesthetic applications at each level of the cognitive taxonomy. Table 4 illustrates how the previously described bodily-kinesthetic abilities could be applied to learning activities at each level of the hierarchy.

3

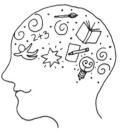

Higher-Order Thinking & Reasoning

Expressing the significance of one's learning using a range of integrated movements (such as gestures, facial expressions, postures, dance, or drama)

↑

2

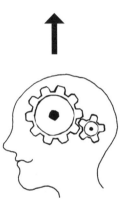

Information Analysis & Processing

Using a complex repertoire of physical skills and coordinated movements to embody and portray one's learning and inquiry

↑

1

Gathering & Understanding Basic Knowledge

Using body movements to mimic others or to create mnemonic links to aid in remembering facts, figures, or concepts

Table 4: Applying the Cognitive Taxonomy to Bodily-Kinesthetic Intelligence

Taxonomy of Cognitive Levels	Bodily-Kinesthetic Abilities				
	Dramatic Enactment	Body Language	Dance & Movement	Skill Performance	Inventing Projects
Higher-Order Thinking & Reasoning **3**	Make connections to contemporary social situations or show personal applications and importance of the information through enactments	Show moods, feelings, inner states of being, beliefs, and values that evoke responses in others, through refined use of the body	Move in ways that are an "interpretive embodiment" or incarnation of the concepts, showing implications and applications	Integrate the skill as part of one's being; show precision performance (unconscious, second-nature execution)	Develop a project in unusual or unexpected ways, showing applications and implications of the basic concepts
Information Analysis & Processing **2**	Show relationships, processes, and dynamics through enactments that include creative embellishments	Show changes, relationships, connections, and processes through a complex repertoire of gestures, facial expressions, and postures	Show multiple layers of understanding and the relationships among pieces of information through a series of well-orchestrated movements	Demonstrate a skill with accuracy and some measure of precision, showing confidence that the skill is known	Develop a project in multidimensional ways, going beyond and creatively applying the basic facts
Gathering Basic Knowledge **1**	Exactly or literally enact, mimic, or portray given facts, events, concepts, or situations	Use gestures, postures, facial expressions, and other body language to literally portray the material, a mood, or other information	Portray feelings, concepts, ideas, and information through a series of simple, isolated, disconnected movements	Demonstrate skills accurately through conscious, careful, step-by-step execution	Incorporate basic facts into a straight-forward, expected development of concepts

Higher-Order Thinking, © 2004 Zephyr Press, Chicago, IL • 800-232-2187 • www.zephyrpress.com

Logical-Mathematical Intelligence Taxonomy
It's as Simple as One, Two, Three

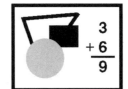

A mathematician, like a painter or poet, is a maker of patterns. If [the mathematician's] patterns are more permanent than theirs, it is because they are made with ideas . . . the mathematician's patterns, like the painter's or poet's, must be beautiful; the ideas, like the colors or the words, must fit together in a harmonious way.

—G. H. Hardy, quoted in *Math for Humans*

For most of us, one of the quickest ways to raise our stress level is to mention mathematics. Many of us associate math with pain. I am still surprised at the number of stories I hear from people in workshops who talk about their scars from inappropriate math tactics applied by well-meaning teachers. In a 1976 article in *MS Magazine,* Sheila Tobias popularized this phenomenon by calling it "math anxiety" (cited in Wahl 1997). Due to the way math is taught in school, we often fail to fully tap the power of this intelligence. A good example is a friend of mine who barely made it through his required math courses in high school. Yet today he is a nuclear engineer in a large East Coast nuclear power plant. Guess what he spends 95 percent of his day doing? Precisely the same math with which he had difficulty in school. But now he does math in context. Now it makes sense because it's relevant to his life in the real world.

In other books I have written I have called the logical-mathematical intelligence the pattern-seeking intelligence. It seeks every conceivable pattern: number patterns, thought patterns, color patterns, traffic patterns, relationship patterns, visual patterns, and so on. It always begins with concrete patterns in the real world, but logical-mathematical thought becomes increasingly abstract as we try to understand relationships in the patterns we have seen. We try to find answers to problems based on or created by the patterns. At this point we resort to using abstract symbols

(such as numbers) to represent patterns we have experienced, to making calculations such as cause and effect or hypotheses, or working with various mathematical formulas to figure out everything from how much paint we need to change the color of our bedroom to how much to tip a server in a restaurant, to figuring out a budget for our family vacation.

For many of us, if math had been taught in context in school, we would have done a lot better and likely would have avoided much of the math anxiety Sheila Tobias discussed. In fact, according to the child development research of Piaget and Inhelder (1969), the earliest developmental stage of what we now call logical-mathematical intelligence is manipulation of and play with a variety of concrete objects in the physical environment and the ability to recognize familiar, previously manipulated objects placed among a range of unfamiliar objects. Children develop the capacity to recognize familiar objects in pictures and to pick those objects out of other pictures containing many other objects that are unfamiliar. Eventually, they are able to imagine objects they have manipulated when those objects are not physically present. This intelligence becomes increasingly abstract and symbolic as it develops. Later in their development children learn about numbers, which are simply abstract symbols representing concrete patterns they have observed. Numbers are what mathematicians call "pure abstractions" because they can be applied to a wide range of objects; namely, you can have 3 women, 3 boats, 3 clouds, 3 mountains, 3 butterflies, and 3 gusts of wind. There are no limits to the 3 symbol. There is no content to the 3 symbol. In and of itself it has no meaning. It gains its significance when used to represent concrete patterns.

Overview of the Logical-Mathematical Taxonomy of Cognitive Abilities

The unique language of the logical-mathematical intelligence is the language of patterns. These recurring patterns include not only traditional mathematical patterns involving numbers, fractions, ratios, or geometric shapes and designs, but also word patterns, visual patterns, sound patterns, even patterns of people or animals. Another feature of logical-mathematical intelligence is patterns of effective problem solving, thinking, and strategizing to meet new challenges. Work with the cognitive abilities for this intelligence involves knowing, analyzing, and processing information in and through the many recurring patterns that surround us in our world and universe. As I mentioned earlier, I feel that Bloom's taxonomy is still the best model we have for understanding the cognitive abilities of the logical-mathematical intelligence.

Here are professions and activities that draw heavily on logical-mathematical intelligence. According to Gardner (1983), it is often in vocational pursuits that we see the ultimate development and potential of the intelligences:

accountants	*businesspersons*
professional debaters	*actuaries*
statisticians	*arbitrators*
math teachers	*underwriters*
computer programmers	*medical professionals*
attorneys	*data analysts*
scientific researchers	*logicians*
bankers	

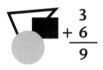

Logical-Mathematical Abilities
The following are the key cognitive abilities of logical-mathematical intelligence

Problem Solving: Employing the tools of the detective to explore and learn concepts of a given discipline. Students learn and have a chance to use a variety of problem-solving techniques and approaches to solve academic problems in various content or subject areas.

Thinking Patterns: Using the full range of thinking skills and thinking models popularized by the so-called thinking skills movement in education. Students work with such techniques as mental menus and cognitive organizers to process and understand curricular material.

Calculation Processes: Learning and using the logical calculation skills unique to each content area. Although this strategy most obviously applies to the content area of mathematics, calculation is a regular part of almost every aspect of our daily lives.

Logical Analysis: Using a complex set of abilities to examine the subtle connections of the various parts of something being studied. Students employ the skills of inductive and deductive reasoning to create convincing arguments for and against issues raised during their studies.

Mathematical Operations: Asking students to move from merely being able to perform a given operation to making it a part of their repertoire for solving daily life problems. In other words, at the higher levels, mathematics moves off the pages of a textbook and becomes a living, useful reality.

Logical-Mathematical Cognitive Taxonomy

The following illustrates general logical-mathematical applications at each level of the cognitive taxonomy. Table 5 illustrates how the previously described logical-mathematical abilities could be applied to learning activities at each level of the hierarchy.

3

Higher-Order Thinking & Reasoning
Using application-oriented mathematical skills and logical thinking abilities, including knowing what thinking skills and patterns to use in a variety of situations

↑

2

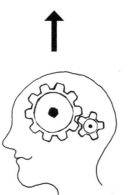

Information Analysis & Processing
Performing standard mathematical calculations and effectively using a variety of problem-solving processes and thinking skills in given content areas

↑

1

Gathering & Understanding Basic Knowledge
Recognizing concrete patterns (sequencing, counting, and so on) and performing simple abstract thinking based on objects

Table 5: Applying the Cognitive Taxonomy to Logical-Mathematical Intelligence

Taxonomy of Cognitive Levels	Logical-Mathematical Abilities					
	Problem Solving	Thinking Patterns	Calculation Processes	Logical Analysis	Mathematical Operations
Higher-Order Thinking & Reasoning 3	Invent new problem-solving strategies, based on but not controlled by previously learned strategies, to solve new problems in new contexts	Employ a wide variety of thinking patterns to show applications, meanings, and implications of certain information	Perform learned calculations in creative and unusual ways to create something new and deal with everyday situations	Find applications or implications that go beyond the provided information to create something new based on it	Apply and integrate mathematical operations to solve problems in every-day life
Information Analysis & Processing 2	Use previously learned problem-solving strategies in new and unexpected ways to meet new challenges in new situations	Use different patterns of thinking in combination to analyze information and reveal relationships, processes, and dynamics	Perform learned calculations on un-known information, showing more fluidity and adaptability than in the previous level	Use analytical meth-ods in unusual and provocative ways to show thinking beyond mere facts; make creative but logical leaps in thinking	Use multiple mathe-matical processes and operations in combination to find solutions to problems
Gathering Basic Knowledge 1	Use problem-solving strategies and methods previously taught (or used) in familiar situations	Use independently several distinct patterns of thinking to show and analyze factual, somewhat obvious information	Perform learned calculations in a textbook, step-by-step manner on given information	Use simple, linear logic to analyze basic facts, figures, and relatively obvious logical aspects of and connections in something	Employ mathematical operations and processes as taught in a textbook or as learned in school

Higher-Order Thinking, © 2004 Zephyr Press, Chicago, IL • 800-232-2187 • www.zephyrpress.com

Naturalist Intelligence Taxonomy
We Are the World!

Time is so precious. I'm under constant pressure from within. Like a volcano, grumbling and rumbling continually. There's thunder and lightning. Ideas and inspiration splash like that. After the rain, eyes can search over life again, washed clean. I try and see with a thousand eyes.

Arthur Shilling, *The Ojibway Dream*

Can you remember powerful experiences you have had out in nature? Maybe you were in your favorite natural setting, or you had an overwhelming experience of nature's power through a spectacular sunset, a mighty storm, or a natural physical formation such as a mountain range or a deep river gorge. Maybe you simply had an unforgettable experience with an animal. Whatever form they take, these experiences of the natural world profoundly affect our sense of well-being and our understanding of who we are and how we fit into the larger patterns of things. The knowings of this intelligence often seem somewhat distant in the so-called concrete jungles where most of us live today.

The naturalist intelligence relates to our recognition, appreciation, and understanding of the natural world around us and the knowings that come from our encounters with it. As an object-related intelligence, the naturalist intelligence deals with the objects of the natural world with which humanity had nothing to do—either with their creation or, in an ideal world, with their continued being. This comment should in no way be interpreted as downplaying the tremendous damage that we humans are doing to the natural world. I am a firm supporter of all organizations and efforts working for conservation, reconstruction, and preservation of the natural resources of this planet on which we are privileged to be living. My comment is instead related to the dynamics and cognitive processes of the naturalist intelligence, which are primarily triggered by patterns, images, designs, colors, textures, smells, tastes, sounds, and other phenomena that occur naturally, with no human intervention.

Overview of the Naturalist Taxonomy of Cognitive Abilities

A quote from Howard Gardner is in order at this point:

> A naturalist is an individual who demonstrates expertise in the recognition and classification of the numerous species—the flora and fauna—of his or her environment. Every culture places a premium on those individuals who can recognize members of a species that are especially valuable or notably dangerous, and can appropriately categorize a new or unfamiliar organism. In cultures without formal science, the naturalist is the individual most skilled in the application of the current "folk taxonomies" (Berlin 1992); in cultures with a scientific orientation, the naturalist is a biologist who recognizes and categorizes specimens in terms of current formal taxonomies, such as those devised by Linnaeus.

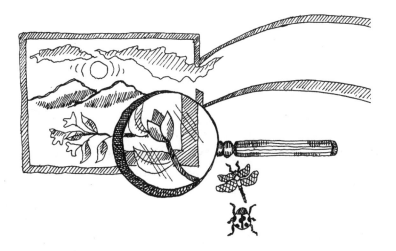

Here are professions and activities that draw heavily on naturalist intelligence. According to Gardner (1983), it is often in vocational pursuits that we see the ultimate development and potential of the intelligences:

forest rangers	*nature guides*
horticulturists	*gardeners*
farmers	*meteorologists*
veterinarians	*life scientists*
animal trainers/keepers	*physical scientists*
florists	*conservationists*

Naturalist Abilities

The following are the key cognitive abilities of naturalist intelligence

Classifying Nature: Recognizing various kinds of groupings of things encountered in the natural environment, including the plant and animal kingdoms, the physical world, and the world of weather patterns. Students learn how to organize natural phenomena into meaningful groups.

Hands-on Investigation: Immersing oneself in the realm of getting to know the natural world firsthand. Generally this occurs through various kinds of experiments, sometimes in a science lab situation, to understand how the natural world operates. However, the investigations can also be part of nature field trips.

Nature Simulations: Creating experiential encounters with the natural world. These often appear in human-created settings; for example, the simulation of a waterfall and stream in a shopping mall. They also include finding ways for nature to have an ongoing impact on one's life.

Caring for Nature: Utilizing the full range of human abilities for respecting, appreciating, and conserving the natural world. Students learn how to make use of nature in such ways that its sensitive ecosystems are not disturbed. This can also include raising, caring for, and training nonhuman creatures.

Natural Patterns: Developing increased levels of awareness and sensitivity to the many patterns of the natural world, both obvious and subtle. This includes not only recognition of distinct patterns, but also understanding the whys and wherefores of those patterns and possible implications and links to patterns in one's own life.

Naturalist Cognitive Taxonomy

The following illustrates general naturalist applications at each level of the cognitive taxonomy. Table 6 illustrates how the previously described naturalist abilities could be applied to learning activities at each level of the hierarchy.

3

Higher-Order Thinking & Reasoning

Making disciplined use of formal taxonomies from biology, chemistry, geology, and other fields to understand, interact with, and respectfully use the natural world

↑

2

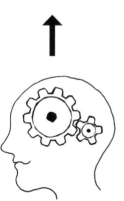

Information Analysis & Processing

Using formal systems for classifying the natural world; using precise methods for investigating nature (such as the scientific method)

↑

1

Gathering & Understanding Basic Knowledge

Being curious about the natural world, including having intuitive, informal schemas of categorization (for example, something is doglike, flower-like, or birdlike)

Table 6: Applying the Cognitive Taxonomy to Naturalist Intelligence

Taxonomy of Cognitive Levels	Naturalist Abilities				
	Classifying Nature	Hands-on Investigation	Nature Simulations	Caring for Nature	Natural Patterns
Higher-Order Thinking & Reasoning — 3	Discern new connections and relationships between the natural world and the human-created world	Design new and creative experiments to test original hypotheses, ideas, and interests	Reveal personal connections to the natural world through abstract, symbolic, or metaphorical representations	Demonstrate a comfort level or unity with conserving the natural world because "It is me"	Grasp connections within connections, see patterns within patterns, almost in a spiritual manner
Information Analysis & Processing — 2	Classify natural phenomena in groupings by subtle features derived from observations of unusual, nonobvious patterns	Conduct extended experiments that are based on and utilize past experiments but move beyond them to new areas of inquiry	Through simulations interpret implications and point out meanings of phenomena observed in the natural world	Embody the spirit of conservation by performing related conservation practices that include but go beyond accepted guidelines	Go beyond previously learned natural patterns to find new patterns based on one's own investigation
Gathering Basic Knowledge — 1	Identify and recognize obvious patterns, groupings, and classifications in the natural world	Conduct experiments that match or reproduce experiments performed by others in the past	Present a literal representation of the basic facts, concepts, and processes observable in the natural world	Follow stated and agreed-on conservation guidelines and principles	Recognize obvious patterns pointed out by other people or contained in written materials

Higher-Order Thinking, © 2004 Zephyr Press, Chicago, IL • 800-232-2187 • www.zephyrpress.com

Using the Object-Related Intelligence Taxonomies: Example Units

The following section outlines three units that illustrate how to move students' thinking to higher-order realms using the object-related intelligences. There are three units, one each appropriate for elementary, middle, and high school. These outlines or synopses are *not* intended to give every detail or enumerate every lesson that would be involved in a given unit. Likewise, I am not suggesting that anyone *should* do these units. Rather, my goal is to illustrate how to use the taxonomies of the object-related intelligences systematically to move students to the higher-order use of the related intelligences and to a higher-order understanding of key curricular concepts. Whether or not your curriculum deems the content I have included to be key concepts is not the point. The point is to show how to use multiple intelligences to get students thinking at higher-order levels in any unit of instruction.

It is not necessary to follow my suggestions in the order listed, although a unit will likely begin with the level of gathering and understanding the basic knowledge (or concepts) of the unit and move up the taxonomies to the higher-order thinking and reasoning level. Although you may not use all the suggestions for each level of the taxonomy, I would suggest you try to balance the learning activities and tasks among the four object-related intelligences. In addition, it is quite possible to mix and match learning activities and tasks such that you might, for example, use visual-spatial intelligence for gathering and understanding basic knowledge and concepts, bodily-kinesthetic for analysis and processing of information, and logical-mathematical for higher-order thinking and reasoning.

Discovering the Key Elements of a Story
A Sample Elementary Language Arts Unit

This unit illustrates ways to tap the object-related intelligences while teaching the elements of a story: characters, setting, plot/action, and themes. The various intelligences and levels of the cognitive taxonomy being tapped are inserted in the outline in bold and summarized in table 7.

- To begin, students create webs showing the various possibilities for each story element. For example, the element of setting could include such aspects as the natural environment, weather conditions, time of day, period of history, and geographic location; the character web might represent facial expressions, moods, descriptions of clothing, culture, race, and age. The goal of the webbing exercise is to help students understand the basic factors that make up each element of a story. **(logical-mathematical intelligence, gathering and understanding basic knowledge)**

- Once they have completed their webs, students break into small expert groups (one group for each of the four elements). In these groups they create a poster illustrating their assigned elements and the various aspects that comprise it. **(visual-spatial intelligence, gathering and understanding basic knowledge)**

- They also create a series of charades to demonstrate physically the various aspects of their assigned element. Each expert group shares their posters and charades with the whole class, explaining the posters and having their classmates try to guess the meaning of the charades. **(bodily-kinesthetic intelligence, gathering and understanding basic knowledge)**

- To illustrate the elements in a story, lead the class in brainstorming a list of their favorite stories about animals or the natural world. Choose one that seems to be familiar to everyone in the class and have the children try to identify the four elements (character, setting, plot/action, themes) of this story. **(naturalist intelligence, gathering and understanding basic knowledge)**

- Working in teams of three, have students pick a favorite story (or you could assign them stories already studied in class). They will analyze the elements of the chosen or assigned story using the object-related intelligences.

- The teams begin by making a four-column chart, labeling one column for each of the four elements. They then write specific examples of the elements from the story in the appropriate columns of the chart. Next they draw lines showing any connections they see across the columns; for example, aspects of the setting that may have an impact on the plot/action or how the characters act. **(logical-mathematical intelligence, analyzing and processing information)**

- The group also analyzes how the natural setting influences the plot and action of the story, including why the author might have chosen that setting **(naturalist intelligence, analyzing and processing information)**

- Then the group creates a diorama that clearly illustrates the various elements of the story and a brief reenactment of the story that explicitly names or demonstrates the various story elements they have been discussing. **(visual-spatial intelligence, bodily kinesthetic intelligence, analyzing and processing information)**

- In the final part of the unit, students apply what they have learned about elements of a story to create a story about their own lives. Using the object-related intelligences, they reconstruct and tell the story of their own life's journey to the present moment.

  ➤ Students begin by brainstorming key animals or natural events that have influenced who they are today (for example, the death of a pet, moving to a new town, the birth of a brother or sister). **(naturalist intelligence, higher-order thinking and reasoning)**

  ➤ They then cluster these items into three chronological groups, forming the three sections or themes of their stories. **(logical-mathematical intelligence, higher-order thinking and reasoning)**

  ➤ Students then create murals that relate their individual stories through pictures, shapes, images, patterns, colors, designs, and textures. The murals are to clearly show the settings, characters, plot/action, and themes of each student's life story and how these elements and factors have contributed to his or her personal journey. **(visual-spatial intelligence, higher-order thinking and reasoning)**

  ➤ Students also create interpretive dances that portray how the various settings, characters, and actions in their life stories have shaped the directions their lives have taken. **(bodily-kinesthetic intelligence, higher-order thinking and reasoning)**

Tips and Preparation for Presenting the Unit

1. Have students practice creating a mural to tell a simple story, such as events that have happened to me today or what I am planning to do over the weekend. Draw a mural of your life's journey as an example.

2. Practice expression through dance prior to the unit. Also practice acting out a topic via charades. Give students opportunities to become comfortable using their bodies to express ideas, emotions, thoughts, and concepts.

3. You may have to spiral the unit and the suggested learning tasks to make them developmentally and grade-level appropriate for your particular students (see Bruner 1966).

4. If students are not familiar with using the graphic organizers suggested for tapping logical-mathematical intelligence, introduce each technique using content from their daily lives; for example, creating webs of what they had for breakfast. Once they have learned the logical thinking pattern, they apply it to the content of the unit.

5. Students may need some instruction on how to create a diorama if this is new to them. Your creating one as an example is likely to be useful.

Table 7: Cognitive Levels and Object-Related Intelligences in Key Elements of a Story Lesson

Cognitive Taxonomy Level	Learning Activities for Object-Related Intelligences
Higher-Order Thinking & Reasoning Students express their own lives as a story using the object-related intelligences as the "story vehicle." Their various story forms must clearly illustrate characters, settings, plot/action, and themes of their life's journey to the present. **3**	**Visual-Spatial:** Students make murals that tell the story of their lives through images, pictures, and visual symbols (including images in the mural story to depict the four elements). **Bodily-Kinesthetic:** Students create dances that tell their life stories to date (include movements that portray characters, settings, plot/action, and themes). **Logical-Mathematical:** Students divide their lives into three phases, then analyze how different characters and settings influenced the theme and plot/action of their life stories. **Naturalist:** Students look at their life's journeys and write about how animals and natural settings have influenced the theme and plot/action of their lives.
Analyzing & Processing Information Students analyze their favorite stories (including movies or TV shows) to identify the four elements and how they were developed. They learn the different ways storytellers use the four elements to create a good story. **2**	**Visual-Spatial:** Students create a diorama illustrating the elements of a favorite story, making sure to include representations for all the elements. **Bodily-Kinesthetic:** With partners, students create a short reenactment of a favorite story, making sure to highlight the four elements. **Logical-Mathematical:** Students create a chart illustrating the logical connections between the four elements in a favorite story (that is, how each element contributes to the whole). **Naturalist:** Students analyze how the natural setting of a favorite story influences the other elements of the story (characters, plot/action, and themes).
Gathering & Understanding Basic Knowledge Students learn the definitions of the four key elements of any story: characters, setting, plot/action, and theme. They learn the details of what is involved in each of the four elements. **1**	**Visual-Spatial:** Students create four posters illustrating the aspects comprising each of the key elements of a story. **Bodily-Kinesthetic:** Students act out each of the four elements using movements that represent each element's key characteristics. **Logical-Mathematical:** Students create story-element webs listing the key or distinguishing features of each element. **Naturalist:** Students remember a story about an animal or one that occurs in a natural setting, then name the four elements in this story.

Higher-Order Thinking, © 2004 Zephyr Press, Chicago, IL • 800-232-2187 • www.zephyrpress.com

Exploring the Metric System
A Sample Middle School Mathematics Unit

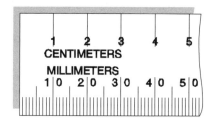

The unit begins with students exploring the metric system through their own bodies. In the next part of the unit, students use the metric system to analyze things that are part of their daily lives. The final stage of the unit involves a "metric system in everyday life" research project. Through using the object-related intelligences, students gain more than just an intellectual understanding of the metric system. They learn to see, imagine, feel, act out, and calculate using metric measurements. The various intelligences and levels of the cognitive taxonomy being tapped are inserted in the outline in bold and summarized in table 8 (page 48).

- Using a meter stick, students measure their own bodies; for example, the length of their legs, arms, and fingers, and how tall they are. They figure out the approximate volume (in cubic centimeters) of their head and their upper body cavity. They figure out their speed (in kilometers) as they walk laps around the school grounds or climb up and down a flight of stairs. They figure (in hectares) the area of the classroom. **(bodily-kinesthetic intelligence, gathering and understanding basic knowledge)**

- Students then read about the metric system (see thc example article on page 45) and create "how much" visuals to accompany the information in the article. Later in the unit, they will use these to help them estimate metric equivalents. **(visual-spatial intelligence, gathering and understanding basic knowledge)**

- Students go out into nature and find objects that approximate the weight, length, and volume of the items listed in the article. They bring these natural objects into the classroom, when appropriate, and place them in a special area where they can be used to aid in metric estimations. **(naturalist intelligence, gathering and understanding basic knowledge)**

- They then create a game to reinforce their understanding and recall of the metric prefixes (such as *centi-, deci-, milli-, kilo-*). Such a game could be based on the formats of popular television game shows; for example, "Metric Prefix Jeopardy," "Metric Concentration," or "Wheel of Metrics." **(logical-mathematical intelligence, gathering and under-standing basic knowledge)**

Metric Measurements

Length

The basic unit of length is the meter.

- The distance from a doorknob to the floor is about one meter.

Millimeter, centimeter, and kilometer are other commonly used units of length.

- The thickness of a dime is about one millimeter.
- The distance across a fingernail is about one centimeter.
- The length of ten football fields placed end to end is about one kilometer.

Mass (Weight)

The basic unit of mass is the kilogram.

- The mass of a football is about one kilogram.

Gram and milligram are other commonly used units of mass.

- The mass of a dollar bill is about one gram.
- The mass of a grain of sand is about one milligram.

Capacity

The basic unit of capacity is the liter.

- Soda pop often comes in two-liter bottles.

Milliliter is another commonly used unit of capacity.

- An eyedropper holds about one milliliter of liquid.

Area

Square centimeter and square meter are commonly used units of area in the metric system.

- A square centimeter measures one centimeter on each side of the square.
- A square meter measures one meter per side.

Volume

The cubic centimeter is a commonly used unit of volume.

- If a cube measuring one centimeter per side were filled with water, the amount of water would be one milliliter. The mass of water would be one gram.
- A cube with a volume of one cubic decimeter measures one decimeter, or ten centimeters, on each side.
- If a cubic decimeter were filled with water, the amount of water would be one liter. The mass of the water would be one kilogram.

Temperature

The Celsius scale is commonly used in countries employing the metric system.

- Water boils at one hundred degrees Celsius.
- Body temperature is thirty-seven degrees Celsius.
- Water freezes at zero degrees Celsius.

Prefixes and Symbols

These are the most common prefixes in the metric system, as well as their symbols and meanings.

Prefix	Symbol	Meaning
mega-	M	million
kilo-	k	thousand
hecto-	h	hundred
deka	da	ten
deci	d	tenth
centi-	c	hundredth
milli-	m	thousandth
micro-	μ	millionth

Following are the official symbols for some common metric measures. (You do not need to use a period or to add an *s* for the plural form.)

m	meter
km	kilometer
cm	centimeter
mm	millimeter
L	liter
ml	milliliter
kg	kilogram
g	gram
m^2	square meter
cm^2	square centimeter
m^3	cubic meter
cm^3	cubic centimeter

Reprinted with permission from David Lazear, *Eight Ways of Knowing* (Arlington Heights, Ill.: Skylight Training and Publishing, 1998).

- Next, students use the metric system to analyze things present in their daily lives. They begin by making a list of things in their lives that are measurable. They will estimate the weight, volume, or area of these things using the metric system. Encourage them to think of fun things to estimate; the more off-the-wall the better! Examples of items to estimate are

  ➤ their weight and height, how many grams they think they can lift, how many kilometers they can run in an hour, the volume of their toes **(bodily-kinesthetic intelligence, analyzing and processing information)**

  ➤ the distance they travel to get to school, the size of pizza their family usually orders, the volume of things in their refrigerator at home (such as milk or orange juice containers), the weight of their favorite sandwich, the area of their pillow **(visual-spatial intelligence, analyzing and processing information)**

  ➤ weights or volumes of items they collect on a field trip to a nearby park or undeveloped area **(naturalist intelligence, analyzing and processing information)**

- They then proceed to test their estimations by weighing or measuring. They learn the formula for translating the metric measurements into their English equivalents (or vice versa). **(logical-mathematical intelligence, analyzing and processing information)**

- Finally, they use a camcorder or digital camera to create a photographic report of their findings entitled "My Metric Life." Each student shares his or her metric documentary with four or five other students. **(visual-spatial intelligence, analyzing and processing information)**

- In the final stage students work in groups to research various applications of the metric system beyond the classroom.

  ➤ Some may decide to investigate careers in which people use the metric system on a daily basis—without converting measurements!

  ➤ Others may want to plan an imaginary trip to countries that use the metric system, researching such things as distances between places they would like to visit, luggage weight allowances on airlines, or the cost of gasoline per liter. **(logical-mathematical intelligence, higher-order thinking and reasoning)**

  ➤ Some may want to make the experience more personal by researching and preparing a report on activities they can do to improve the quality of their own lives, such as losing weight or analyzing their diet—using the metric system, of course! **(bodily-kinesthetic intelligence, higher-order thinking and reasoning)**

- Students research the components of a healthy diet including the amounts (in metric) of various foods they should eat, as well as their cardiovascular exercise needs. They use this information to plan and track their healthy lifestyles. (**naturalist intelligence, higher-order thinking and reasoning**)

- The culmination of students' research projects is a metric fair where they visually display their research findings. (**visual-spatial intelligence, higher-order thinking and reasoning**)

Tips and Preparation for Presenting the Unit

1. Some parts of the unit need to occur out of doors. Carefully plan a location where students can quickly get into the measuring and estimating task. Make sure there is enough material there for them to work with.

2. Practice expression of ideas and concepts through visual representation prior to the unit so that students build their comfort level with this means of communicating. You may want to go on a brief tour of the school, looking for visuals that communicate information (for example, pictures identifying the men's and women's restrooms, the circle with a diagonal line through it indicating that something is prohibited).

3. You may want to create a simple metric-system board game to give students ideas for creating their own games. Also have students try out the games they create on the class. A great deal of learning can occur through a game. You may even decide to expand the games as students move to other levels of the unit.

4. When students are estimating what they can do with their bodies, it may be best to move to a large space allowing movement, such as the gym or school grounds.

Table 8: Cognitive Levels and Object-Related Intelligences in Exploring the Metric System Lesson

Cognitive Taxonomy Level	Learning Activities for Object-Related Intelligences
Higher-Order Thinking & Reasoning Students research where the metric system is used in practical, daily living (such as in medical and scientific careers and in metric-using countries). They imagine themselves operating effectively in these situations. **3**	**Visual-Spatial:** Students create visual displays or exhibits showing the metric system in use (a pharmacist filling a prescription, a scientist doing an experiment, and so on). **Bodily-Kinesthetic:** Students prepare a complete report on their bodies using only metric measurements (for example, current and ideal weights). **Logical-Mathematical:** Students plan a trip to a metric-using country and calculate all aspects of the journey in metric values (kilograms of luggage allowed or kilometers between cities visited). **Naturalist:** Students plan healthy diets for themselves using metric measurements (grams of the different food groups allowed or cardiovascular activity in meters).
Analyzing & Processing Information Students participate in a wide range of measuring and estimating exercises where they learn how to measure and recognize distance, volume, and area in metric terms. **2**	**Visual-Spatial:** Students create a photographic or video "metric report" of their lives (distance to grandparents' house, weights of family members, or the area of their bedroom). **Bodily-Kinesthetic:** Students use metric measurements to estimate various activities they can perform with their bodies, then test their estimates (how many centimeters they can jump or how many grams they can lift). **Logical-Mathematical:** Students learn how to convert nonmetric measurements into metric and vice versa, applied to measurements they already know. **Naturalist:** On a field trip, students estimate measurements of objects in nature using the metric system, then test their estimates.
Gathering & Understanding Basic Knowledge Students learn the definitions of the key terms of the metric system and their nonmetric equivalents. They also learn the meanings of the metric prefixes (*kilo-, centi-, milli-,* and so on). **1**	**Visual-Spatial:** Students create visuals to accompany "how much" descriptions for the different metric measures (see page 45). **Bodily-Kinesthetic:** Students turn their bodies into metric measuring instruments by figuring out the length of their arms, the volume of their head, or how fast they can walk laps around the school grounds. **Logical-Mathematical:** Students learn the meanings of the metric prefixes and create a logic game to practice using the prefixes. **Naturalist:** Students gather objects from nature to use in estimating metric measurements (the weight of a rock or the length of a branch).

Higher-Order Thinking, © 2004 Zephyr Press, Chicago, IL • 800-232-2187 • www.zephyrpress.com

Europe in the Middle Ages
A Sample High School History Unit

This unit begins with students working in various "expert groups" to understand key characteristics of life in the Middle Ages, with each group assigned a different topic area. The various intelligences and levels of the cognitive taxonomy being tapped are inserted in the outline in bold and summarized in table 9 (page 52).

- Each group researches their assigned area and uses a different graphic organizer to present information to the rest of the class. Possible graphic organizers could be Venn diagrams comparing and contrasting different classes of society; webs showing various socioeconomic factors (such as commerce, agricultural base, economy, or populations); tree charts showing political structures; or timelines sequencing key events, trends, and historical stages. **(logical-mathematical intelligence, gathering and understanding basic knowledge)**

- Each group also creates a mural or some other pictorial way to display the information they have collected. **(visual-spatial intelligence, gathering and understanding basic knowledge)**

- Groups of students may also create natural-world simulations of natural phenomena people faced during the Middle Ages. **(naturalist intelligence, gathering and understanding basic knowledge)**

- Finally, they create a mini-drama in which they act out the real-life implications of what they have been studying (For example, a day in the life of a man, woman, and child.). **(bodily-kinesthetic intelligence, gathering and understanding basic knowledge)**

- The groups then share their graphic organizers, visual representations, and dramatic enactments with the rest of the class.

- Working in groups again, students choose various research projects to further explore medieval life.

  ➤ One group, for example, could study the paintings and sculptures produced in this period and try to represent something from their life today using the artistic styles of the Middle Ages. They discuss how and why their creations are represented differently from how they would be expressed in modern times. **(visual-spatial intelligence, analyzing and processing information)**

> ➤ Another group could study dance forms and drama from the period. They experiment with learning the dances and producing the dramas, reflecting on the differences between these art forms and their contemporary counterparts. (**bodily-kinesthetic intelligence, analyzing and processing information**)

> ➤ Another group could explore how the natural world affected and shaped life in a typical medieval village and report their findings by creating a large diorama of a village and its environment. (**naturalist intelligence, analyzing and processing information**)

> ➤ Another group could use Webs or other graphic organizers to compare and contrast life in the Middle Ages versus the twenty-first century. (**logical-mathematical intelligence, analyzing and processing information**)

- Students could exhibit the products from these explorations as a Middle Ages museum for the entire student body to view.

- Students identify environmental and natural concerns of people in the Middle Ages, then compare and contrast those issues to the ones we face in contemporary society. (**naturalist intelligence, higher-order thinking and reasoning**)

- To culminate the unit, lead the class in a visualization in which they journey back in time, imagining they are living in a medieval village. Ask them to explore how their lives are different from life in the twenty-first century. (**visual-spatial intelligence, higher-order thinking and reasoning**)

- When they return from their imaginary journey, they form groups and pretend they are going to produce a television show based on the realities of medieval life. They choose a contemporary TV show and recreate it as if it were taking place in the Middle Ages, making appropriate changes to reflect the issues, concerns, problems, and situations relevant to people in that period. They record their shows with a camcorder and present them to the rest of the class with the contemporary episodes on which they were based. (**bodily-kinesthetic intelligence, higher-order thinking and reasoning**)

- Lead the entire class in a final reflection on the Middle Ages by having them discuss the pluses, minuses, and interesting features of living in the Middle Ages from the perspective of the twenty-first century. Chart the features. (**logical-mathematical intelligence, higher-order thinking and reasoning**)

Tips and Preparation for Presenting the Unit

1. Have students first practice creating a mural to tell a story, for example, about things that have happened to them today or what they are planning to do over the weekend. Do a mural of your life's journey as an example.

2. Practice expression through dramatic enactment prior to the unit so students become comfortable (and willing) to express ideas, emotions, thoughts, and concepts in front of their peers. It may be best to have students practice in small groups initially. Structure the activity like charades, where they draw a piece of paper out of a hat and act out the situation written on it for their partners. Then move them into acting out things from the Middle Ages.

3. You may need to review or teach the various graphic organizers suggested for the logical-mathematical parts of the unit. When teaching a thinking skill, first teach the pattern using a topic that is easy, fun, and related to daily life (such as classifying the clothes students own, or comparing and contrasting themselves with their siblings). Once students understand the logical thinking pattern, then apply it to the content of the unit.

4. In order for students to make successful dioramas, make sure you have supplies on hand such as clay, construction paper, glue, and paints. Have each group bring a box from home in which to build the village. Begin by discussing where students have seen dioramas in the past. Ask them to reflect on how the diorama affected them or helped them more fully understand a topic. Such a preliminary discussion will help diffuse comments that dioramas are elementary school stuff.

5. If students are not familiar with guided imagery or visualization processes, you might begin with several short experiences, such as asking them to create a mental picture of how their bedroom looked when they left it that morning. Have them describe to a partner what they are seeing in as much detail as possible. Then practice a more complex visualization by taking them on an imaginary trip from the school to the downtown area of your city or town. Again, the goal is to give students a chance to practice "seeing with the mind's eye" before you take them back in time.

6. You may need to enlist some outside help with filming the Middle Ages TV shows. This could very possibly be the most exciting part of the unit and the one that most deepens and expands students' learning about this period of history.

Table 9: Cognitive Levels and Object-Related Intelligences in Europe in the Middle Ages Lesson

Cognitive Taxonomy Level	Learning Activities for Object-Related Intelligences
Higher-Order Thinking & Reasoning Students reflect on how their lives would be different if they were living in the Middle Ages. They list the pros and cons of living in the Middle Ages and show how the Middle Ages have influenced our lives in the twenty-first century. **3**	**Visual-Spatial:** Students participate in a visualization exercise in which they travel back in time to the Middle Ages, experiencing how things would be different from today. **Bodily-Kinesthetic:** Students revise and act out a segment of a TV show as if it had been created in the Middle Ages. Students videotape their segments, then play the contemporary show and the videotape one after the other. **Logical-Mathematical:** Students create a chart showing pluses, minuses, and interesting features of life in the Middle Ages from the perspective of the twenty-first century. **Naturalist:** Students compare and contrast twenty-first century environmental concerns and issues with those faced by people living in the Middle Ages.
Analyzing & Processing Information Students learn to analyze medieval art and drama for distinguishing characteristics of life in the Middle Ages. They do a sociological analysis of this period of history and its impact on people living then. **2**	**Visual-Spatial:** Students try to represent modern themes using painting or sculptural styles from the Middle Ages, exploring how themes, concerns, or interests unique to this period influence their representations. **Bodily-Kinesthetic:** Students study medieval dramas or dances and enact portions that illustrate key themes of this period. **Logical-Mathematical:** Students create a series of webs analyzing similarities and differences between aspects of life in the Middle Ages and in the twenty-first century. **Naturalist:** Groups create dioramas of a medieval village, focusing on the natural setting in which people lived and how this setting shaped their lives.
Gathering & Understanding Basic Knowledge Students learn about distinguishing characteristics of life in Europe during the Middle Ages, including the social structure, art and drama, and natural environment (including diet, agriculture, livestock). **1**	**Visual-Spatial:** Students create murals depicting all aspects of life during the Middle Ages. **Bodily-Kinesthetic:** Students create mini-dramas showing a day in the life of a woman, a child, and a man in each of the classes of medieval society. **Logical-Mathematical:** Students make a series of Venn diagrams comparing and contrasting different topic areas (such as what it was like to be a serf, a nobleman, and members of other classes in the medieval social system). **Naturalist:** Students create virtual, natural-world simulations of what natural phenomena they would have had to deal with if they were living in the Middle Ages.

Higher-Order Thinking, © 2004 Zephyr Press, Chicago, IL • 800-232-2187 • www.zephyrpress.com

3

The Object-Free
Forms of Intelligence

"Object-free" forms of intelligence . . . are not fashioned or channeled
by the physical world but, instead, reflect the structures of particular
languages and music. They may also reflect features of the auditory
and oral systems, though . . . language and music may each develop,
at least to some extent, in the absence of these sensory modalities.
—Howard Gardner, *Frames of Mind*

In his original research on multiple intelligences, Howard Gardner (1983) categorized the musical-rhythmic and verbal-linguistic intelligences as *object-free*. They are called object-free because their modes of cognitive processing do not rely on objects, real or imagined, that have an independent existence in the external world or the world of the imagination.

Consider a musician composing or performing a piece of music or an author writing a poem. What is produced is not a thing in the traditional sense. It exists rather in the realm of tones, rhythms, beats, vibrational patterns, pitch, timbre, volume, and tempo. The poet uses language to conjure images of things, but the words themselves contain nothing! Rather, poetry consists of dealing with intangibles such as nuances, syntax, metaphor, grammar, analogy, tense, phonetics, and simile. Via the spoken and written word, imaginary realities may be created that have no physical counterparts in the world of physical objects. Musical-rhythmic and verbal-linguistic intelligences are triggered by the structures and patterns of particular languages and sounds, as well as by all the complex features and possibilities of the human auditory and oral systems.

In lessons or units that use the taxonomies of the object-free intelligences, we are really operating within realms that explore the power of language to create impressions of reality, inspire, motivate, or move us to action, as well as the evocative power of sound and vibration. To be successful, you must crawl inside these intelligences' unique ways of knowing, understanding, and learning, and open yourself to processing information within their unique cognitive realms, which are not based on concrete objects in the real world that you can taste, touch, smell, or see.

Musical-Rhythmic Intelligence Taxonomy
The Hills Are Alive with Sound

Music is:

> *bonding with nature*
> *allowing creativity to express itself*
> *refreshment of the spirit*
> *a development of the spiritual within us*
> *getting in touch with eternal flow*
> *resurgence of self*
> *reconvening of life*
> *spiritual bonding*
> *involvement—an "at-oneness" with the rhythm of living*
> > —Barbara Crowe, quoted in *Music: Physician for Times to Come*

In my recent book *The Intelligent Curriculum,* I commented that the musical-rhythmic intelligence probably has a stronger consciousness-altering effect than do any of the other intelligences. We use music, rhythm, sound, or vibration to instantly shift our mood or awareness. Many of us will play certain kinds of music when we are stressed out and need to calm down and other kinds of music to energize ourselves when we're feeling lethargic, bored, or otherwise down. Some music is used as a background for routine tasks such as cleaning the house or working on a project. Culturally, we use music, rhythm, sound, and vibration to express love for another person, deep loss and grief, or ecstatic joy. We use music, rhythm, sound, and vibration to express religious devotion or national pride, and to celebrate our various cultural backgrounds. A television or movie soundtrack plays a crucial role in enhancing our experience of the show. Advertisers also use music, rhythm, sound, and vibration when trying to persuade consumers to purchase their products.

A number of researchers suggest that this intelligence would better be called the *auditory-vibrational intelligence,* for it goes far beyond music and rhythm. One reason for this suggestion is an awareness of how many things people know simply by listening to the sounds around them. Can you tell when something is wrong with your car from the way it sounds (even if you don't know what's wrong)? What can you tell about the weather from listening to what is happening outside? When you are talking with another person, or listening to others converse, how much do you learn simply from listening to the tone and pitch of their voices and the rhythm patterns of their speech? Often the music, rhythm, and tone of a person's speech communicate his or her state of being more accurately than the meaning of the words and phrases they speak.

A number of years ago I was conducting a workshop for the faculty of a school in West Virginia. When introducing musical-rhythmic intelligence, I usually lead people through an exercise in which they listen to snippets from several very different kinds of music. As they listen, I have them write down the impact the music is having on them; namely, what feeling it evoked. One of the teachers in the workshop was a teacher of profoundly deaf children and was herself profoundly deaf. Prior to this session I struggled with how I could enable her to participate in this exercise. Finally, just before the session, I hit on the idea of having her "listen" to the beat and vibration of the various musical pieces. I had her sit by the boom box and place her palms on the speakers. The result blew my mind: She had very similar responses to the music from feeling the vibrations as did those who could hear.

Musical-rhythmic (or auditory-vibrational) intelligence is a very powerful way of knowing, one whose potential I believe we have just barely scratched the surface of in public education. In and through this intelligence, I believe we come in contact with the rhythm and beat of life itself—a rhythm and beat that surges just beneath the surface of every aspect of life, if we would just stop and listen.

Overview of the Musical-Rhythmic Taxonomy of Cognitive Abilities

In the workshops I conduct for businesspeople and educators, participants often become nervous when we start working with this intelligence. I will frequently hear comments like "I have no sense of rhythm!" or "I have no musical ability. I can't even carry a tune!" In the first instance, so-called musical ability has little or nothing to do with this intelligence, for we are dealing with a way of knowing that makes use of sound, rhythm, tone, beats, and vibration. We all have this intelligence! It is part of our physiology and neurology as human beings. The following taxonomy is designed to help you explore and rediscover this very important part of yourself and to empower those dimensions of this intelligence that may not be as well developed as others.

Here are professions and activities that draw heavily on musical-rhythmic intelligence. According to Gardner (1983), it is often in vocational pursuits that we see the ultimate development and potential of the intelligences:

> *sound engineers*　　*radio broadcasters*
> *advertisers*　　*singers/performers*
> *musicians*　　*sound effects specialists*
> *music teachers*　　*musical directors*
> *soundtrack creators*　　*instrument makers and repairers*
> *songwriters*

Musical-Rhythmic Abilities
The following are the key cognitive abilities of musical-rhythmic intelligence

Creating Music: Using a variety of musical forms to accompany learning of various concepts. Examples are using music as a mnemonic device or employing the more creative and evocative aspects of music to expand understanding and deepen personal connections with learning.

Sound Illustrations: Expressing concepts, thoughts, feelings, and ideas through various sounds. This strategy is akin to the use of sound illustrations in old-time radio shows to make the show more real for listeners. Students learn to use and create appropriate sounds to enhance their understanding of the material they are studying.

Auditory Links: Creating "sound metaphors and similes" for concepts being learned. Students learn how to make meaningful associations between concepts they are studying and a full range of auditory experiences and media.

Musical Structures: Using a range of different forms, kinds, and schemas of music to create meaningful associations with material being learned. The strategy ranges from very obvious associations (such as music from a certain culture) to use of musical schemas to evoke a response in someone else.

Auditory Patterns: Using such qualitative and quantitative aspects of sound as timbre, volume, pitch, or tempo to create emotional connections with information being learned. Students use sounds they and others make to create an auditory interpretation of what they are learning.

Musical-Rhythmic Cognitive Taxonomy

The following illustrates general musical-rhythmic applications at each level of the cognitive taxonomy. Table 10 illustrates how the previously described musical-rhythmic abilities could be applied to learning activities at each level of the hierarchy.

3

Higher-Order Thinking & Reasoning
Using music, rhythm, sound, and vibration to integrate, synthesize, or transfer new learning or concepts into one's repertoire for living

2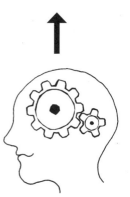

Information Analysis & Processing
Employing various tonal qualities and patterns, rhythms, beats, and other forms of sound to enhance learning and understanding

1

Gathering & Understanding Basic Knowledge
Using music, rhythm, sound, and vibration to aid memory and recall of specific pieces of information, facts, and figures

Table 10: Applying the Cognitive Taxonomy to Musical-Rhythmic Intelligence

Taxonomy of Cognitive Levels	Musical-Rhythmic Abilities					
	Creating Music	Sound Illustrations	Auditory Links	Musical Structures	Auditory Patterns
Higher-Order Thinking & Reasoning **3**	Create a seamless concept soundtrack that orchestrates original or borrowed music, rhythms, and sounds	Use multiple sounds to create an auditory mirror or auditory reflection on information being learned	Create new auditory links between specific subject matter and existing compositions, or create new auditory compositions to embody personal insights	Create musical forms or structures that convey feelings, thoughts, ideas, and concepts and evoke those responses in others	Make interpretive use of auditory and vibrational patterns to convey ideas, thoughts, and emotions
Information Analysis & Processing **2**	Combine original music, rhythms, and sounds with those created by someone else to create concept-appropriate accompaniments	Employ an array of interesting, creative sounds to create auditory connections or associations with certain information	Make unusual, surprising, and unexpected links between learning and the auditory realm	Understand nonobvious connections between musical forms and concepts, emotions, and thoughts	Use a full repertoire of auditory embellishments to suggest subtle relationships and connections within a topic being studied
Gathering Basic Knowledge **1**	Employ simple composition techniques based on music, rhythms, and sounds created by someone else	Use obvious and expected sounds to suggest or accompany certain concepts or situations	Make obvious links between material being learned or situations being portrayed and certain music, rhythms, and sounds	Recognize simple connections between a musical form and a concept or life situation	Mimic music, rhythms, and sounds that are directly related to specific topics, concepts, or situations

Higher-Order Thinking, © 2004 Zephyr Press, Chicago, IL • 800-232-2187 • www.zephyrpress.com

59

Verbal-Linguistic Intelligence Taxonomy
Just Say the Word

The deep structure of any given language embodies a particular syntax of perception, and to the extent an individual develops the deep structure of his native language, he simultaneously learns to construct, and thus perceive, a particular type of descriptive reality, embedded, as it were, in the language structure itself. From that momentous point on . . . the structure of his language is the structure of his self and "the limits of his world."
—Ken Wilber, *The Atman Project*

According to some researchers, at birth we possess the capacity to learn any of more than three thousand different languages, but we are not born proficient in any of them. When we begin to interact with the primary language in our environment, the brain can already recognize all the sounds of the language. The language networks in our brain, through cultural patterning, frequency of hearing, repeated attempts to mimic these sounds (and probably our own survival instincts as well), usually cause us to develop only one or two of these potential languages into full-blown, sophisticated language systems. Words are powerful! They can evoke emotion; they can move people to act on an issue; they can make us laugh; they can produce feelings of hatred; they can heal.

Verbal-linguistic intelligence involves all forms of working with language, including reading the newspaper, a novel, or the labels on various products we buy; writing essays, poetry, reports, or letters; formal speaking before an audience and informal conversation with a friend; and listening to someone's words and understanding both what they are saying and what they are intending to communicate. This is probably the most familiar intelligence to people in the Western world. Most of us spend the majority of our waking hours using the verbal-linguistic intelligence. It is also strongly emphasized in all our systems of public education.

One of the most interesting (and challenging!) aspects of working with verbal-linguistic intelligence is that a person may be strong and proficient in using and delivering the spoken word while at the same time being less than proficient with the written word, or vice versa. And even within the realms of spoken and written language, a person may have various levels of proficiency; for example, being able to write beautiful and flowing poetry but unable to write a clear, logical paragraph, or being able to deliver a rousing, persuasive speech but unable to give a coherent set of step-by-step instructions for performing a routine task.

Overview of the Verbal-Linguistic Taxonomy of Cognitive Abilities

In some ways the taxonomy of cognitive abilities for verbal-linguistic intelligence encompasses the four major processes at work in the human brain whenever we are involved in speaking, reading, or writing.

Semantics: Understanding individual word meanings is called semantics. As an author, I often struggle for days to find the right words to convey precisely the meanings I am trying to communicate. Semantics is even more important for poets, who may struggle not only with word meanings but with shades of meaning and shades of shades of meaning. The realm of semantics also encompasses figures of speech such as metaphors, similes, hyperbole, analogy, and symbolic language.

Syntax: Understanding the order of words and how that order affects their meaning within the context of other words is called syntax. (For example, "The cat bit the dog" has a very different meaning from "The dog bit the cat.") At the heart of the syntactic process is the culturally agreed-on logic of a given language system. Syntax involves such things as making sure there is subject-predicate agreement and clear antecedents, ensuring prepositions have objects, and avoiding dangling participles.

Praxis: Understanding word meanings within different social and cultural contexts is known as the praxis (or practical usage) of a language. Praxis encompasses cultural nuances, idioms, and how words and phrases are used in different sociocultural situations. At one time in my life I taught English as a second language and ran head-on into the difficulty of explaining certain idioms of American English to foreign speakers. How would you explain such phrases as "run that by me again" or "speaking to a full house"?

Phonetics: How words are pronounced is called phonetics. Under phonetics I also include intonation and inflection. Often the way something is said communicates more about the speaker's intended meaning than the literal meaning of the words. Take a statement such as "She looks nice today" and see if you can alter its meaning simply through the tone, pitch, timbre, and emphasis of your speech. How would you say it with sarcasm? With pity? With admiration? With envy?

These four processes are at the heart of teaching language. When working with the verbal-linguistic taxonomy, I feel it is important continually to underscore these four areas so that students become more aware of what is involved in reaching a deep level in this intelligence, which they often take very much for granted.

Here are professions and activities that draw heavily on verbal-linguistic intelligence. According to Gardner (1983), it is often in vocational pursuits that we see the ultimate development and potential of the intelligences:

lecturers	*comedians*
authors	*literary agents*
poets	*publishers*
editors	*debaters*
journalists	*copyists*
reporters	*teachers*

Verbal-Linguistic Abilities
The following are the key cognitive abilities
of verbal-linguistic intelligence

Creative Writing: Using the various techniques, styles, and genres of written language to express one's dialogue with and understanding of concepts under study. Included are such things as vocabulary, sentence and paragraph structure, nuances of expression, and grammatical complexity.

Poetic Expression: Using the many different forms of poetry to represent learning, understanding, and applications of what one has learned. This strategy encompasses all the myriad possibilities of expression present in poetic metaphor, simile, meter, and free and rhyming verse.

Formal Speaking: Expressing thoughts, feelings, and ideas in and through the different forms of oral language, including storytelling, persuasion, extemporaneous speaking, and the "how to" speech. Students learn how to articulate their understandings and the implications of what they are studying.

Linguistic Humor: Using the full range of linguistically based humor, including plays on words, unexpected endings, satire, parody, hyperbole, and various other twists of language that express different levels of understanding.

Listening and Reporting: Intently listening to and understanding the message of another person or persons. Students develop and use such skills as empathy for perspectives that differ from their own, the ability to paraphrase what someone has said, and understanding implied meanings in others' messages.

Verbal-Linguistic Cognitive Taxonomy

The following illustrates general verbal-linguistic applications at each level of the cognitive taxonomy. Table 11 (page 64) illustrates how the previously described verbal-linguistic abilities could be applied to learning activities at each level of the hierarchy.

3

Higher-Order Thinking & Reasoning
Articulating implications or applications of new information
in terms of oneself or one's larger social context

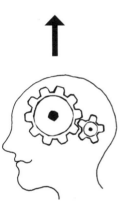

2

Information Analysis & Processing
Using the various styles, genres, and techniques of a language to analyze
one's understanding or feelings about certain information, or its significance

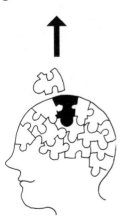

1

Gathering & Understanding Basic Knowledge
Learning about a topic, concept, or subject area by reading,
writing, and speaking about the relevant information

Table 11: Applying the Cognitive Taxonomy to Verbal-Linguistic Intelligence

Taxonomy of Cognitive Levels	Verbal-Linguistic Abilities				
	Creative Writing	Poetic Expression	Formal Speaking	Linguistic Humor	Listening & Reporting
Higher-Order Thinking & Reasoning **3**	Use a wide variety of writing techniques and genres to express one's original thoughts and feelings as well as those of others	Use poetry as a vehicle to express thoughts, feelings, and understandings regarding certain information, oneself, and the world	Explore the larger implications of the material and its connections to other learning and knowledge	Based on certain topics or concepts, create a humorous routine involving clever, witty use of language	Demonstrate deep listening to and assimilation of a presentation by reporting on "what I've learned"
Information Analysis & Processing **2**	Employ a variety of writing forms and styles to express one's wrestling with and digestion of certain material	Employ a variety of poetry techniques to demonstrate thoughtful processing of material under study	Discuss basic information by pondering its meaning or raising questions about its significance	Use material or concepts as a jumping off place for humorous speaking or writing	Report on the subtle aspects of a presentation and on personal conclusions drawn from it
Gathering Basic Knowledge **1**	Use a limited repertoire of basic writing forms to convey simple understandings and ideas	Use elementary rhyme or poetic rhythm patterns to express simple facts and figures related to a topic	Give a simple speech in which the basic facts, figures, and information are presented with little elaboration	Use very obvious, expected humor related exactly to the concepts under study	Report very basic information communicated in another's presentation

Higher-Order Thinking, © 2004 Zephyr Press, Chicago, IL • 800-232-2187 • www.zephyrpress.com

Using the Object-Free Intelligence Taxonomies: Example Units

The following section outlines three units that illustrate how to move students' thinking to higher-order realms using the object-free intelligences. There are three units, one each appropriate for elementary, middle, and high school. These outlines or synopses are *not* intended to give every detail or enumerate every lesson that would be involved in a given unit. Likewise, I am not suggesting that anyone *should* do these units. Rather, my goal is to illustrate how to use the taxonomies of the object-free intelligences systematically to move students to the higher-order use of the related intelligences and to a higher-order understanding of key curricular concepts. Whether or not your curriculum deems the content I have included to be key concepts is not the point. The point is to show how to use multiple intelligences to get students thinking at higher-order levels in any unit of instruction.

It is not necessary to follow my suggestions in the order listed, although a unit will likely begin with the level of gathering and understanding the basic knowledge (or concepts) of the unit and move up the taxonomies to the higher-order thinking and reasoning level. Although you may not use all the suggestions for each level of the taxonomy, I would suggest you try to balance the learning activities and tasks among the two object-free intelligences.

Exploring the Continents of Our World
A Sample Elementary Geography/Social Studies Unit

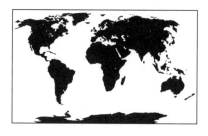

In this elementary geography/social studies unit, students study the continents using musical-rhythmic and verbal-linguistic intelligences. The unit begins with students compiling basic information about the continents. Next they analyze and research assigned continents. In the final part of the unit, they reflect on the gifts and contributions to the world that come from each continent. The various intelligences and levels of the cognitive taxonomy being tapped are inserted in the outline in bold and summarized in table 12 (page 68).

- Students learn the names of the continents, listen to songs from various continents, then modify the lyrics from one to create a song incorporating the names of the continents and one distinguishing characteristic of each one. **(musical-rhythmic intelligence, gathering and understanding basic knowledge)**

- Divide the class into seven groups and assign each one a continent, or have them draw the name of a continent out of a hat. (To allow for more groups, you could have an eighth group research the island nations of the South Pacific.) Give each group a fact sheet containing key information the students need to learn about their assigned continent. They study the facts in their groups, then compose a poem about their assigned continent. The poem is to use the information they have studied and present it in such a way that someone reading the poem would learn key information about the continent. They then share their poems with the rest of the class. **(verbal-linguistic intelligence, gathering and understanding basic knowledge)**

- Have the continent groups further analyze and research their assigned continent, maybe via Internet searches to learn information about such things as climate, geological features, population, religions, animals, customs, food, economic base, and vegetation. They turn their research into an audio tape recording, perhaps in the form of an old-time radio show. The recordings are to be complete with appropriate sound effects, background music, and people speaking the language(s) of the continent. The goal is to give listeners an auditory experience of the continent. **(musical-rhythmic intelligence, analyzing and processing information)**

- As part of the research, encourage students to read stories, poetry, and plays from the continent, and to analyze what they can learn about the continent from its literature. **(verbal-linguistic intelligence, analyzing and processing information)**

- When the groups have completed their research, have them share their shows with the whole class and list things that are similar and different among the continents of the world.

- Students choose the continent they find the most interesting (other than the one they studied in their group). They write a story about how their lives would be different if they were growing up on the chosen continent. As they write, they are to incorporate information they have learned from their own research and the research of their classmates. **(verbal-linguistic intelligence, higher-order thinking and reasoning)**

- Students create a soundtrack to accompany stories they write about the continents. The soundtrack should be reminiscent of what they have learned about the continents. **(musical-rhythmic intelligence, higher-order thinking and reasoning)**

Tips and Preparation for Presenting the Unit

1. For the higher-order story-writing task, it may be useful to have prepared several "scenario-starters" to help students begin their scenarios. For example, "A typical day in my life if I had grown up on the _____ continent . . ."

2. You may wish to gather music from the different continents, preferably children's songs with words. This will make it easier for students to learn the songs, then change the words to incorporate facts about the continents.

3. Likewise, you will need to do some background research to find appropriate literature from the different continents. Look for a variety of forms: poems, stories, and plays.

4. When students start recording their radio shows, you will need a quiet recording room and probably some outside help to save on time. Also be ready to coach the children in thinking of possible sound illustrations for their continent. Having a box of sound makers may help them get started.

Table 12: Cognitive Levels and Object-Free Intelligences in Continents of Our World Lesson

Cognitive Taxonomy Level	Learning Activities for Object-Free Intelligences
Higher-Order Thinking & Reasoning Students research how their lives have been influenced and shaped by contributions originating in the different continents. **3**	**Musical-Rhythmic:** Students create a soundtrack to accompany stories they write about the continents. The soundtrack should be reminiscent of information they have learned about the continents. **Verbal-Linguistic:** Students write stories describing how their lives would be different if they were growing up on a different continent, taking into consideration their probable socioeconomic situation, employment of family members, schooling, and religion.
Analyzing & Processing Information Students compare and contrast what life would be like on each continent based on such factors as climate, food, animal life, vegetation, terrain, or rainfall. **2**	**Musical-Rhythmic:** Each group of students is assigned a continent. They create an audio tape that illustrates, via sound, the climate, animal life, vegetation, and so on. The class notes which sounds are common among several continents. **Verbal-Linguistic:** Students read stories, poetry, plays, and other literature from the different continents, noticing how they are different and similar, and what they can learn about the continent through its literature.
Gathering & Understanding Basic Knowledge Students learn the names of the continents, their shapes, where they are on a world map, and key distinguishing facts and characteristics of each. **1**	**Musical-Rhythmic:** Students learn songs from the different continents, then create new lyrics to rehearse and remember the key facts about each continent. **Verbal-Linguistic:** Students choose a continent from a hat and must make up a poem about the continent that communicates its most important distinguishing characteristics and how it's unique.

Higher-Order Thinking, © 2004 Zephyr Press, Chicago, IL • 800-232-2187 • www.zephyrpress.com

Understanding the Human Circulatory System

A Sample Middle School Science/Health Unit

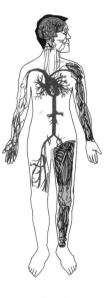

In this unit students learn about the human circulatory system, beginning with the basic functions and definitions of the circulatory organs. The various intelligences and levels of the cognitive taxonomy being tapped are inserted in the outline in bold and summarized in table 13 (page 71).

- Students read about the circulatory system and make a list of the organs involved and their various functions. Working in groups, they make up riddles, jokes, or limericks about the organs and their functions in the circulatory process, which they share with the class. **(verbal-linguistic intelligence, gathering and understanding basic knowledge)**

- Assign each small group to invent a sound analogy for a particular circulatory organ; for example the sound of blood getting oxygenated or the sound of the different chambers of the heart receiving and pumping out the blood to the rest of the body. The teams share their sound analogies with the rest of the class, explaining why and how each is an appropriate sound for the assigned part of the system. Then they create a mini-symphony of circulation by having the groups produce the sounds for each of the organs. You act as a conductor, pointing to various groups to make their sounds on cue. **(musical-rhythmic intelligence, gathering and understanding basic knowledge)**

- Bring anything you can find that will allow students to hear and monitor the process of circulation, such as stethoscopes, biofeedback machines, or blood pressure cuffs. Give them time to learn how to use the instruments to listen to the sounds of the circulatory system. Have them experiment with ways to alter the sounds; for example, running in place for three minutes, then listening again. What new sounds are they hearing? What has changed? **(musical-rhythmic intelligence, analyzing and processing information)**

- Students experiment with listening to different kinds of music and sounds and notice their effects on the circulatory system; for example, what effect does a soothing lullaby have on breathing and heart rates? What happens with a rousing march? What about sounds from nature, such as waves crashing on a shore? What about the sound of a jack-hammer tearing up a street? **(musical-rhythmic intelligence, analyzing and processing information)**

- Have students write a story entitled "A Day in the Life of the Heart" (or one of the other organs involved in circulation). For example, they might create "My Journey through the Circulatory System" as if written by a red blood cell. Have students share in small groups the stories they have written. Have each group select one to share with the whole class. **(verbal-linguistic intelligence, analyzing and processing information)**

- In the final part of the unit, students work in groups to create info-mercials about steps people can take to ensure their circulation is good and stays healthy for a long time, such as getting regular exercise and eating a proper diet. **(verbal-linguistic intelligence, higher-order thinking and reasoning)**

- They also create soundtracks of music, rhythms, tones, and beats to accompany their infomercials. **(musical-rhythmic intelligence, higher-order thinking and reasoning)**

- When they have completed their presentations, set up a time to record each with a camcorder. Let students play their infomercials on a television for the rest of the class.

- Ask students to write a brief paper on what they have learned about themselves in the unit and what changes they want to make in their lifestyles to take better care of their circulatory systems. **(verbal-linguistic intelligence, higher-order thinking and reasoning)**

Tips and Preparation for Presenting the Unit

1. Enlist the help of medical and health professionals in the community in gathering the instruments for monitoring the various sounds of the circulatory system.

2. When you get to the point of filming the infomercials, you will probably want to enlist the aid of the school's audiovisual professional, a parent with a camcorder, or other person.

3. Make sure to provide tape recorders so students can record the soundtracks for their infomercials separately. This will allow them to focus on doing the infomercial well rather than being distracted with the soundtrack elements.

Table 13: Cognitive Levels and Object-Free Intelligences in Understanding the Circulatory System Lesson

Cognitive Taxonomy Level	Learning Activities for Object-Free Intelligences
Higher-Order Thinking & Reasoning Students do an inventory of various environments, diets, and kinds of exercise to determine which are most conducive to healthy circulation, including an inventory of factors related to their own circulatory systems and how to improve them. **3**	**Musical-Rhythmic:** Students make up and record on a cassette recorder soundtracks to accompany infomercials about how to maintain a healthy circulatory system. **Verbal-Linguistic:** Students create a series of infomercials about what they should do to care for their own circulatory systems. The infomercials are to incorporate everything they have learned about the circulatory system. To close, they write about changes they want to make in their own lives.
Analyzing & Processing Information Students analyze the various factors that promote a healthy circulatory process, including what can go wrong if one does not care for and nurture those organs. **2**	**Musical-Rhythmic:** Using medical instruments, students learn to monitor the circulatory system. They experiment with ways to change heart and breathing rate, including running in place, and with the effects of listening to and producing different kinds of music, rhythms, sounds, and vibrational patterns. **Verbal-Linguistic:** Students write stories about the circulatory system as a whole or from the perspective of various organs involved in circulation; for example, "A Day in the Life of the Heart."
Gathering & Understanding Basic Knowledge Students learn the names of the organs involved in the circulatory system, the role of each, and how they work in synergy to create a healthy, functioning organism. **1**	**Musical-Rhythmic:** Students create series of sounds, rhythms, beats, and tones as analogies for what takes place in the various organs during the various stages of circulation. They combine these to create a symphony of circulation. **Verbal-Linguistic:** Students create riddles, limericks, and jokes about the different circulatory organs and the stages of circulation.

Shakespeare for Today
A Sample High School English Literature Unit

In this high school English literature unit, students study several plays by William Shakespeare in expert groups. They use musical-rhythmic and verbal-linguistic intelligences to deepen their understanding and appreciation of the plays. The unit leads to each expert group recasting their play for modern times. The various intelligences and levels of the cognitive taxonomy being tapped are inserted in the outline in bold and summarized in table 14 (page 74).

- The unit begins with students working in three expert groups. Each group thoroughly studies one play: *Macbeth, Hamlet,* or *Romeo and Juliet.* As they read the plays in their groups, they keep a log of phrases, expressions, and words that are characteristic of Elizabethan English—maybe those they do not fully understand! (**verbal-linguistic intelligence, gathering and understanding basic knowledge**)

- Have students research the meanings of these phrases, expressions, and words and write their own definitions of what they mean. (**verbal-linguistic intelligence, gathering and understanding basic knowledge**)

- They then create a rap or song about Elizabethan English, which they share with the rest of the class. The songs should incorporate the archaic words and expressions as well as explain their meanings. (**musical-rhythmic intelligence, gathering and understanding basic knowledge**)

- Continuing to work in their expert groups, they begin a careful analysis of their assigned play. They study the classical structure of a Shakespearean drama. They analyze the main characters for temperament, backgrounds, motives, and archetypal representations. They analyze the motifs present in the play and discuss the universal appeal of these themes; for example, where in movies, television shows, or stage plays are these themes represented today? (**verbal-linguistic intelligence, analyzing and processing information**)

- For each character, they create a musical theme that embodies some of what they have learned about the character, similar to the way each character has a distinctive theme in Prokofiev's *Peter and the Wolf.* They also study the use of sound effects and musical instruments in the staging of a Shakespearean drama. (**musical-rhythmic intelligence, analyzing and processing information**)

- Each group writes a short drama derived from their assigned play, exploring the various motifs, social situations, and interplay of the characters in a contemporary setting (see the tips below for assistance). If they wish, they can base the story on current events; for example, Microsoft's battle to maintain control of its products. **(verbal-linguistic intelligence, higher-order thinking and reasoning)**

- They design their plays like mini–Broadway musicals by incorporating contemporary songs to drive home the themes being explored; characters' motives, feelings, or thoughts; and commentary on the general social situation. They may also use instrumental background music to enhance the drama by building suspense, or lightening the mood. **(musical-rhythmic intelligence, higher-order thinking and reasoning)**

- The unit concludes with the groups staging their productions for each other. Students reflect on the unit by writing about how these archetypal characters and universal themes are familiar in their lives today. **(verbal-linguistic intelligence, higher-order thinking and reasoning)**

Tips and Preparation for Presenting the Unit

1. To help students generate ideas for their contemporary dramas, brainstorm different types of shows they could create and what they could do in that context; for example, a talk show with Lady Macbeth as a guest, a sitcom about the Montagues and the Capulets, or "Wheel of Fortune" with Hamlet as Pat Sajak and his mother as Vanna White.

2. Before they write their contemporary dramas, encourage students to put the Shakespearean characters in contemporary situations and see how things would play out; for example, *A Midsummer Night Dream*'s approach to the War on Terrorism.

Table 14: Cognitive Levels and Object-Free Intelligences in Shakespeare for Today Lesson

Cognitive Taxonomy Level	Learning Activities for Object-Free Intelligences
Higher-Order Thinking & Reasoning Students write a short play based on their assigned play, recasting it in modern times. They stage these productions for the rest of the class. **3**	**Musical-Rhythmic:** Students create a soundtrack for a mini-drama based on their assigned play, using contemporary songs to drive home the universal themes and message of the play. **Verbal-Linguistic:** Students write a mini-drama that sets a Shakespearean play in modern times, incorporating contemporary concerns, issues, and problems and showing how the play's characters might react and what they might do. They reflect on the universal themes and archetypes in the play.
Analyzing & Processing Information Students analyze the universal themes and archetypal figures represented in a play and begin to make connections with where these figures appear in modern media and how they are portrayed. **2**	**Musical-Rhythmic:** Students study the staging of a Shakespearean play and how the sound effects were made. They imagine what a modern soundtrack might sound like, inventing themes to represent each character. **Verbal-Linguistic:** Student analyze the various characters in the drama and relate them to similar characters in contemporary theater, television, or movies. They also trace the key themes of their play and how those themes show up in modern dramas.
Gathering & Understanding Basic Knowledge Students study one drama, learn the meanings and etymology of various expressions in Elizabethan English, and identify their equivalents in modern times. **1**	**Musical-Rhythmic:** Students take a list of Elizabethan phrases they have encountered in reading a play and create raps or songs using these phrases in such a way that their meanings are clear. **Verbal-Linguistic:** Students read a play and make a list of unfamiliar phrases, expressions, words, and ways of speaking in Elizabethan English. Then they research the meanings and origins of these words and phrases.

Higher-Order Thinking, © 2004 Zephyr Press, Chicago, IL • 800-232-2187 • www.zephyrpress.com

4

The Personal Forms of Intelligence

The personal forms of intelligence reflect a set of powerful and competing constraints: the existence of one's own person; the existence of other persons; the culture's presentations and interpretations of selves. There will be universal features of any sense of person or self, but also considerable cultural nuances, reflecting a host of historical and individuating factors.

—Howard Gardner, *Frames of Mind*

Interpersonal and intrapersonal intelligences contain in their names Howard Gardner's final classification of the intelligences. They are called the personal intelligences for at the heart of both is the individual's life as a person. In the case of interpersonal intelligence, the focus is our lives in relationship with one another. In the case of intrapersonal intelligence, the focus is one's life as a solitary, self-reflective creature. In many ways these intelligences are two sides of a single coin. Some of our greatest learning and discoveries about ourselves happen when we are working with or playing with others as part of some collaborative effort. But it is also true that those things we know deeply about ourselves we can fairly safely assume are also true of others—once we get through the many layers of our personalities, we arrive at a core self in which there are many more similarities than differences!

The interpersonal and intrapersonal intelligences tend to draw on all the intelligences as they go about their unique ways of knowing. Consider interpersonal intelligence for a moment and all that is involved in relating to or working with other people: We talk (verbal-linguistic); we use visuals to enhance the meaning of our words (visual-spatial); we employ gestures, facial expressions, and postures to help others experience what we are trying to communicate (bodily-kinesthetic). The tone, pitch, and rhythm of our speech often communicate more than the actual meaning of the words we use (musical-rhythmic); and there are certain logical rules we follow, both in the proper use of the language and in the act of communication itself (logical-mathematical).

In the case of intrapersonal intelligence, consider the difficulty we often experience in adequately expressing the depth of our self-knowledge. To compensate, we often resort to the world of symbols to help us point to the profound within our own lives. In other words, we try to give expression to our inner wrestling, wisdom, and soul through art, drama, music, dance, poetry, or sculpture. We make analogies and seek connections between our routine daily lives and the archetypal patterns and powerful phenomena of the natural world.

When working with the taxonomies of the personal intelligences, we must couch the various learning tasks and activities in person-related frameworks; on the one hand, people relating to other people, and on the other, a person relating to him- or herself.

Interpersonal Intelligence Taxonomy
Getting to Know You

Passing over . . . entering sympathetically into other lives and times . . . is the way to completeness. This is not an unlikely hypothesis. For whenever a man passes over to other lives or other times, he finds on coming back some neglected aspect of his own life or times which corresponds to what he saw in the other's. Passing over has the effect of activating these otherwise dormant aspects of himself. If he were to stay fixed on himself, fixed on his own standpoint from which to survey all things . . . he would never experience his own wholeness.

—John Donne, *The Way of All the Earth*

The stuff of the interpersonal intelligence is the stuff of human relationships and relating, be it one-on-one with another person, as part of a team (or some other type of cooperative effort), or simply as an informal evening chatting with close friends in your living room. In some ways I believe that the educational research into cooperative learning and how to make it work represents the state-of-the-art research on interpersonal intelligence. In fact when we look at the core operations or capacities associated with the interpersonal way of knowing, they are almost identical to what cooperative learning calls the social skills: such skills as deeply listening to the communication of others, doing your part in a team effort, encouraging and supporting others in your group, understanding and appreciating others' diverse perspectives (especially when they differ from one's own), and empathy.

Most of us spend a huge part of each day relating to and working with others. We are part of different kinds of teams in the workplace. We serve on committees in organizations to which we belong. Many of the most important things we have learned in our lives we learned in and through formal and informal relationships with other people. Because we spend so much time relating to and working with others, I really believe we often take interpersonal intelligence for granted, thinking it is second nature. But is it? How skillful really are we in relating? How much do we really value and understand everything that is involved in deep cooperation and collaboration with others? Beginning in early childhood, throughout our formal schooling, and into our adult work life, the normal socialization process in most Western societies provides us with hundreds of formal and informal training opportunities in how to be competitive and how to stand as a "rugged individual." Because of this conditioning, it often takes a dramatic experience to bring home to us the importance of knowing how to work effectively with others.

For about the first twenty years of my professional life, I worked with an international human development organization that was doing rural development in developing countries. The organization would send out small teams of people, usually two or three families, to work with people in village situations who had extended an invitation to work with them. I learned more about effective interpersonal relationships (and intelligence) in this work than in anything else I have done in my life. The organization was self-supporting, so some members of the team had to get jobs, and they pooled their income, giving all members of the team small monthly stipends for personal living expenses. The remainder was used for the needs of the team: food, shelter, medical expenses, utility expenses, and so on. We all lived in the same house, which became our staff residence. Most meals were taken in common. All decisions were made by consensus. I can remember times when we sat around a table for hours, trying to hammer out a consensus everyone could live with and for which everyone could take responsibility. We did not allow ourselves to vote, for voting tends to split the solidarity of a team. After the vote you have two camps: those who were for, and those who were against, the decision.

While I am not suggesting that such a radical step is the only way to become deeply rooted in the interpersonal intelligence, it does involve putting yourself or your students in a situation of positive dependence on others; that is, "We sink or swim together!" The interpersonal capacities of cooperation and collaboration are very different from those of competition and individualism. A key finding of all cooperative learning research also supports one of the key factors for enhancing and strengthening this intelligence: We must explicitly teach students the social skills of cooperation and collaboration.

Overview of the Interpersonal Taxonomy of Cognitive Abilities

The intelligence corollary to the need to explicitly teach students the social skills of collaboration is that we must consciously and diligently exercise and practice using the core capacities of interpersonal intelligence if we are to strengthen it within ourselves. Therefore, when we are working with the cognitive abilities of interpersonal intelligence, we must be passionate first and foremost about involving students in great experiences of cooperative learning—experiences where as a group they clearly achieve more than they could on their own. Creating authentic "we sink or swim together" situations in the classroom will very quickly move students up the interpersonal taxonomy to high-level functioning in this intelligence.

Here are professions and activities that draw heavily on interpersonal intelligence. According to Gardner (1983), it is often in vocational pursuits that we see the ultimate development and potential of the intelligences:

counselors   *organization leaders*
teachers   *talk show hosts*
therapists   *public relations managers*
politicians   *sociologists*
receptionists   *customer service representatives*
mediators   *human resources managers*
social workers   *consultants*
anthropologists

Interpersonal Abilities

The following are the key cognitive abilities
of interpersonal intelligence

Empathetic Processing: Stepping inside another person's perspective, so to speak, in order to understand his or her thoughts, feelings, motivations, behaviors, or moods. Doing so does not necessarily imply agreement with that person, but it does imply an understanding and appreciation of where he or she is coming from.

Giving Feedback: Giving another person accurate and meaningful feedback based on a genuine understanding of the kind of feedback that will help the person. This ability also involves helping another person understand and apply the feedback.

Listening to Others: Not only deeply listening to and understanding another person's message, including being able to repeat what the person said in a way that honors the meaning and implications of the communication, but also being able to interpret the message to another person.

Team Building: Tapping the full range of collaborative skills involved in any serious group effort or cooperative learning situation, ranging from simply doing the tasks or jobs assigned in a group to taking full responsibility for the success of the team as a whole and of each member of it.

Inquiry and Questioning: Asking questions that tap information recall but go beyond the facts to probe for genuine understanding, creative thinking, and real-life applications of the information.

Interpersonal Cognitive Taxonomy

The following illustrates general interpersonal applications at each level of the cognitive taxonomy. Table 15 illustrates how the previously described inter-personal abilities could be applied to learning activities at each level of the hierarchy.

3

Higher-Order Thinking & Reasoning
Using an in-depth understanding of human relationships and group-process dynamics to build group consensus, manage conflict, and develop profound levels of human caring and sensitivity

↑

2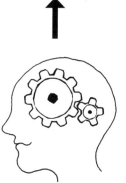

Information Analysis & Processing
Employing relatively sophisticated relationship and interpersonal skills to probe for understanding in others and to promote more meaningful human relationships among other people

↑

1

Gathering & Understanding Basic Knowledge
Using basic interpersonal skills such as listening, doing one's part in a team or group effort, and encouraging others

Table 15: Applying the Cognitive Taxonomy to Interpersonal Intelligence

Interpersonal Abilities

Taxonomy of Cognitive Levels	Empathetic Processing	Giving Feedback	Listening to Others	Team Building	Inquiry & Questioning
Higher-Order Thinking & Reasoning — 3	Speak wholly from the perspective of the partner, trying to justify, amend, or expand on the partner's responses	Give feedback through a genuine dialogue with teammates in which responses are probed and examined for thorough understanding	Accurately interpret another's communication and act on or use this communication	Take full responsibility for the team, not only doing own part but also assisting others in doing their parts	Identify an accurate response by questioning to ensure that the answerer truly understands the concept
Information Analysis & Processing — 2	Communicate an answer/response given by a partner, and include some of the partner's perspective on its accuracy	When giving feedback, ask teammates to expand on and more fully explain their initial responses/ answers	Understand meanings and implications of what another says	Go beyond the initial guidelines to do more than strictly required in a co-operative group	Recognize an accurate response to a question even when the response is phrased differently from the way the concept was originally presented
Gathering Basic Knowledge — 1	Accurately repeat an answer/response given by a partner	Relate feedback and evaluation to whether or not the information matches the information originally given	Repeat accurately what another has said	Do own part in a cooperative group exactly as outlined by the teacher	Evaluate an answer based on how closely it resembles the form in which the original information was given

Higher-Order Thinking, © 2004 Zephyr Press, Chicago, IL • 800-232-2187 • www.zephyrpress.com

Intrapersonal Intelligence Taxonomy
What's It All About?

If one holds oneself dear,
one should diligently watch oneself . . .

One should first establish oneself
in what is proper;
then only should one instruct others.
Thus the wise man
will not be reproached . . .

One truly is the protector of oneself;
who else could the protector be?
With oneself fully controlled,
one gains mastery
that is hard to gain.

—Buddha, *The Dhammapada*

Intrapersonal intelligence involves the whole range of activities we employ to figure out who we are as human beings and what is the meaning, purpose, and significance of our lives. The research behind this intelligence has focused on the cognitive, neurological, and psychological processes involved in any kind of serious introspection. This intelligence encompasses anything dealing with internal aspects of the self, such as one's feelings, beliefs, values, self-identity, and questions and answers about life goals.

See if you can recognize this process in your life: When you are alone, what non-work-related thinking do you really enjoy? What do you do for personal renewal? When you are stressed, angry, or anxious, what practices do you use to alter your consciousness or awareness? In the last year, what new discoveries have you made about yourself that in some way altered your previous self-understanding? If you had to answer the question, "Who am I really?" and you couldn't talk about external appearances, skills you've acquired, relationships you have with others, or your work, what would you say? What do you do when you need inspiration or when you need to spark your own creativity? What process do you use to evaluate yourself and your goals? What personal growth and development activities are you currently involved in or have you tried in the recent past? The stuff of intrapersonal intelligence is the stuff of self-awareness, self-reflection, and being in touch with the inner world of our individual being.

As far as we know, humans are the only creatures who possess self-consciousness, the ability to step back from ourselves, reflect on the self, and learn from our reflection. In *The Intelligent Curriculum*, I made the following observations, which bear repeating here:

> Intrapersonal intelligence is . . . the least understood of all of the eight intelligences, the least valued in our Western world, and often it is feared and considered to be dangerous. Why is this? Part of the problem comes from the fact that a great deal of the work of this intelligence occurs deep within the human psyche; therefore, we have no "external product" to show for this work, and we are a product-driven society! Another part of the problem is that the bias of all Western societies favors verbal-linguistic and logical-mathematical intelligence; namely, "If you can't write about it, talk about it, and logically explain it to someone else, it has no real value." Many of our intrapersonal knowings can not be adequately communicated in these verbal-linguistic or logical-mathematical forms. I also have noticed that we tend to be afraid of this area of intelligence. Have you noticed how we feel we must have some form of external stimulation to keep us entertained almost every waking hour? And how we hesitate to take the time to look deeply into the self, probably out of fear over what we might discover lurking behind the closed doors of our psyche? (Lazear, 2000, 38)

We have all had experiences that are profound beyond words and logic. I grew up in Wyoming, far from any ocean. I can still remember the first time I encountered the ocean, in California, standing on the shores of the mighty Pacific. It was like an immense opening happened in me. It was as if for the first time in my life, I realized that I was part of this phenomenon and it was part of me! It was almost like a spiritual experience. And I remember how profoundly moved I was and how frustrated I was as I tried to communicate the depth of this encounter to my family. It was almost as if the whole experience turned to meaningless drivel as it rolled off my tongue. I realized then that for some events and happenings in our lives, language just doesn't hack it! Some experiences are beyond words!

The products that are produced by intrapersonal intelligence tend to be "inner products" and thus are sometimes difficult to communicate to others. They are nonetheless critical to our well-being as human creatures and to students' deep and lasting learning in the school setting. Some of the products and benefits of this way of knowing for students include genuine self-reflection, the finding or creation of meaning in what they are studying (a critical part of deep learning and understanding), and the making of connections between what they are learning and life beyond school.

Overview of the Intrapersonal Taxonomy of Cognitive Abilities

We have at least two concerns when we work with the taxonomy of cognitive abilities for intrapersonal intelligence. One is how to provide easy, non-threatening ways for students to make their inner worlds of the self visible to others. More important is to help them get in touch with their own deepest concerns, values, and beliefs. Therefore, our main concern is to promote self-reflection. At the lower levels of the taxonomy, self-reflection basically involves becoming consciously aware that we have this capacity. As we move up the taxonomy, however, we have the possibility of leading students into an awareness of their awareness—what current researchers call the process of metacognition.

Here are professions and activities that draw heavily on intrapersonal intelligence. According to Gardner (1983), it is often in vocational pursuits that we see the ultimate development and potential of the intelligences:

spiritual counselors
psychologists
human potential researchers
clergy
meditation guides
mental health professionals
philosophers
psychiatrists
cognitive patterns researchers
religious leaders
therapists

Intrapersonal Abilities
The following are the key cognitive abilities
of intrapersonal intelligence

Self-Reflection: Dealing with the unique human capacity to step outside oneself, so to speak, to look back at the self, almost as an outside observer. Doing so involves development of the skills of self-analysis, discerning personal implications of something being learned, and appropriate application of one's learning to practical challenges and problems of daily living.

Emotional Processing: Making affective connections between oneself and the life situations and contexts of other people, including being aware of the emotional impact of one's own and others' thoughts, actions, and words.

Metacognition: Literally, "thinking about thinking." This ability involves becoming highly aware of one's own thought processes, including knowing about different patterns of thinking, analyzing one's own thinking strategies, and knowing how to develop stronger thinking skills in oneself and others.

Values Clarification: Using the ability to examine the larger picture; namely, understanding what really matters in relation to the larger contexts of life—the community, the nation, the world, the cosmos—beyond oneself as an isolated individual.

Self-Identity: Developing a deep sense of self, not only at the level of obvious, superficial aspects, but also at the profound levels where we examine such issues as the meaning, purpose, and significance of our lives in the overall scheme of things.

Intrapersonal Cognitive Taxonomy

The following illustrates general intrapersonal applications at each level of the cognitive taxonomy. Table 16 illustrates how the previously described intrapersonal abilities could be applied to learning activities at each level of the hierarchy.

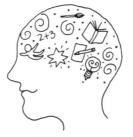

3

Higher-Order Thinking & Reasoning

Developing an intimate awareness of the process of being self-conscious (deeply conscious about all aspects of oneself as a being) and how to extend this awareness to all aspects of daily life

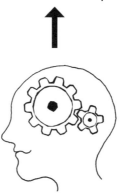

2

Information Analysis & Processing

Employing somewhat profound understandings of the self, including knowledge about the various processes of the self and the dynamics of self-consciousness

1

Gathering & Understanding Basic Knowledge

Becoming aware of rudimentary aspects of the self, such as physiological needs, emotions, and personal likes and dislikes

Table 16: Applying the Cognitive Taxonomy to Intrapersonal Intelligence

Intrapersonal Abilities

Taxonomy of Cognitive Levels	Self-Reflection	Emotional Processing	Metacognition	Values Clarification	Self-Identity
Higher-Order Thinking & Reasoning **3**	Transform the original information or concept into a profound articulation of self-discovery and even reevaluation of self-identity	Be deeply moved in fairly complex ways by the subject matter; subject matter reveals new aspects of the self or one's life	Interest oneself more in problem-solving procedures than in getting the "right" answer (very aware of own thinking processes)	Express many potential shifts in values, priorities, self-understandings, and personal philosophy	Express multiple levels of analogical self-understanding in and through self-reporting
Information Analysis & Processing **2**	Go beyond obvious and expected implications to articulate new learning, insights, discoveries, or reflections	Express several levels of emotional response, indicating an understanding of deeper human motives	Talk about inter-mediate steps and thinking employed between the "text-book steps" of problem solving (understand the purpose of the steps)	Make numerous connections to the self via feelings, questions raised, or things that are personally interesting	Show a number of creative or surprising connections between the concepts and own life
Gathering Basic Knowledge **1**	See some connections and surface/obvious implications based on factual information about the concept	Articulate surface, "expected" feelings or emotions, showing basic personal con-nections with the material	Accurately restate the textbook steps for getting the right answer (with little or no understanding of the purpose of these steps)	Accurately report basic facts about a topic but sees little or no impact of the information on the self	Identify with the obvious, surface aspects of the subject, topic, or concept

Higher-Order Thinking, © 2004 Zephyr Press, Chicago, IL • 800-232-2187 • www.zephyrpress.com

Using the Personal Intelligence Taxonomies: Example Units

The following section outlines three units that illustrate how to move students' thinking to higher-order realms using the personal intelligences. There are three units, one each appropriate for elementary, middle, and high school. These outlines or synopses are *not* intended to give every detail or enumerate every lesson that would be involved in a given unit. Likewise, I am not suggesting that anyone *should* do these units. Rather, my goal is to illustrate how to use the taxonomies of the personal intelligences systematically to move students to the higher-order use of the related intelligences and to a higher-order understanding of key curricular concepts. Whether or not your curriculum deems the content I have included to be key concepts is not the point. The point is to show how to use multiple intelligences to get students thinking at higher-order levels in any unit of instruction.

It is not necessary to follow my suggestions in the order listed, although a unit will likely begin with the level of gathering and understanding the basic knowledge (or concepts) of the unit and move up the taxonomies to the higher-order thinking and reasoning level. Although you may not use all the suggestions for each level of the taxonomy, I would suggest you try to balance the learning activities and tasks among the two personal intelligences. Remember that the personal intelligences tend to use all the other intelligences in the act of relating to and with other people and reflecting on the self, so it is fine to have students draw pictures, act things out, sing, or write an essay as long as the focus is on enhancing the knowing that occurs through interpersonal relating and intrapersonal introspection!

Understanding the Water Cycle
A Sample Elementary General Science Unit

In this unit students learn about the water cycle and why and how it is important for life on our planet. For most of the unit, students work in cooperative groups, then do personal reflection on what they have learned in their groups. For the analyzing and processing information segments of the unit, you will need some way to give students a virtual experience of the entire process of the water cycle, from the raindrop falling initially to its eventual return to the atmosphere (see the tips on page 90 for suggestions). The final stage of the unit examines how the water cycle is in jeopardy today due to humans' lack of care for this vital resource. The intelligences and levels of the cognitive taxonomy being tapped are inserted in the outline in bold and summarized in table 17 (page 91).

- The unit begins with students learning the basic vocabulary needed to discuss the water cycle, including definitions of the various stages. They look up the dictionary or textbook definitions; then, in cooperative groups, they rewrite the definitions in their own words. They also create illustrations to accompany the definitions. **(interpersonal intelligence, gathering and understanding basic knowledge)**

- Students close their eyes and remember experiences they have had with water. They pretend they have a television inside their heads on which they can view a movie of their water experiences. After several minutes of this inner remembering, each turns to a partner and describes the experience, *using the newly learned vocabulary words* to relate the experience. **(intrapersonal intelligence, gathering and understanding basic knowledge)**

- After a "virtual experience" of the water cycle (see "Tips and Preparation for Presenting the Unit" on page 90), divide students into expert groups, with each group assigned to one stage of the water cycle. In their expert groups, they are to take their assigned stage and learn as much as they can about it. Team members are given assignments such as doing Internet searches, going to the library, and interviewing other people to investigate thoroughly the stage they have been assigned. Each expert group prepares a report on what they have discovered in their investigations and shares it with the rest of the class. **(interpersonal intelligence, analyzing and processing information)**

- Students individually reflect on the importance of the whole water cycle to them through activities such as journaling about why the water cycle is important to them personally or what might happen if the cycle were missing a stage. They share their reflections with a partner. **(intra-personal intelligence, analyzing and processing information)**

- In their expert groups, students research conservation efforts and other measures being taken to protect our water resources. Their research culminates in the creation of a water cycle and water conservation display to share with other classes and perhaps with parents at a special time. **(interpersonal intelligence, higher-order thinking and reasoning)**

- To close the unit, have students think about and plan things they can do in their own lives and within their families to conserve and protect Earth's water resources. **(intrapersonal intelligence, higher-order thinking and reasoning)**

Tips and Preparation for Presenting the Unit

1. The definitions of terms and the stages of the water cycle may come directly from your general science textbook. The point of the first stage of the unit is for students to become conversant with the meanings of the terms so they can comfortably (and intelligently) use them in normal conversation.

2. For a virtual reality experience, you could use such things as filmstrips or videos that illustrate the stages of the water cycle. You could also take students to a science and industry museum that has displays about the water cycle. Field trips to places where some of the stages of the water cycle can be observed firsthand would also be appropriate.

3. When the expert groups are researching their assigned stages, your role as the teacher is to help them get in touch with the information. This will probably require you to do some advance research on the Internet or in the library. You might make some calls to professionals in the community to see if they would be willing to have students interview them. Although students are to do the actual research, you will probably have to jump-start the process.

4. For the culminating display, coordinate with other teachers and the principal to work out the best venue. It may fit into a parent-teacher conference time or perhaps be part of a special parent or community night.

Table 17: Cognitive Levels and Personal Intelligences in the Understanding the Water Cycle Lesson

Cognitive Taxonomy Level	Learning Activities for Personal Intelligences
Higher-Order Thinking & Reasoning Students research how the various stages of the water cycle affect life on the planet and what they can do to help conserve and protect this precious resource. **3**	**Interpersonal:** Still working in expert groups, students do research projects to find out how the different stages of the water cycle affect human life, how this resource is being destroyed, and what people are doing to protect our world's water supply. They create displays to share with parents and other classes. **Intrapersonal:** Students create plans for water conservation and protection in their own lives, and for more careful, respectful use of water in their families.
Analyzing & Processing Information Students investigate the various stages of the water cycle, learning what takes place at each stage and why it is important to the whole cycle. **2**	**Interpersonal:** Working in expert groups students research a specific stage of the water cycle, learning about all the processes involved and why they are important for the whole cycle. They prepare a report to teach what they have learned to the rest of the class. **Intrapersonal:** Students journal about why each stage of the water cycle is important to them personally or about what would happen if a stage suddenly disappeared. They share their reflections with a partner.
Gathering & Understanding Basic Knowledge Students study and learn the definitions of words needed to understand and talk about the water cycle (for example, *condensation, precipitation*) and reflect on personal experiences they have had with these events. **1**	**Interpersonal:** In cooperative groups, students look up basic definitions of the relevant vocabulary; then as a team they write, in their own words, the meaning of each term, including an accompanying illustration. **Intrapersonal:** Students remember personal experiences related to the water cycle (such as a rainstorm when camping, watching the morning dew evaporate, steam condensing on the bathroom mirror after they took a hot shower) and use newly learned vocabulary to describe these to a partner.

Volcanoes and Me
A Sample Middle School Earth Science Unit

The unit begins with students studying the history of volcanic activity on earth and the role volcanoes have played in shaping the earth's present physical characteristics. Next students research how volcanoes work and they plan museum-style displays to present their findings. In the final part of the unit, students study and learn about the impact of volcanoes on society. The intelligences and levels of the cognitive taxonomy being tapped are inserted in the outline in bold and summarized in table 18 (page 94).

- In small groups, students learn about the geological results of volcanic activity, including types of volcanic rocks and land formations, how to recognize signs of volcanic activity, and how volcanic activity has shaped the earth. They share any personal experiences they have had with volcanoes and of the land formations they now know result from volcanic activity. **(interpersonal intelligence, gathering and under-standing basic knowledge)**

- Students also spend some time thinking and journaling individually about what they know about volcanoes and any questions they hope to have answered during the course of the unit. They share with the class what they want to learn about volcanoes. **(intrapersonal intelligence, gathering and understanding basic knowledge)**

- Show videos or films of recent volcanic eruptions, such as those of Kilauea (in Hawai'i) or Mount St. Helens (in Washington State).

- Working in cooperative groups of four to six, have students research the geological processes involved in the formation and eruption of a volcano. Assign two research topics to each small group, and have the group decide how to divide up and assign the work (probably in pairs or trios). Encourage the groups to use the Internet and library resources, to contact volcano research and monitoring institutions around the world, or to conduct interviews to gather their information. **(inter-personal intelligence, analyzing and processing information)**

- Each pair or trio of students devises a research plan for creating a museum-style display to report to the class on their investigations. Each pair or trio shares their plan first within their small group, then with you to get feedback and suggestions (see the tips below for suggested displays). Each pair/trio completes the project, then evaluates its effectiveness as a learning tool. **(intrapersonal intelligence, analyzing and processing information)**

- Working again in expert groups, students research past and recent volcanic eruptions such as Vesuvius in Pompeii, Mount Etna in the south of Italy, or the eruption of Mount Pinatubo in the Philippines. Have them gather news stories, historical accounts, video footage (where available), and other materials to demonstrate the results of their assigned eruption. In their research they are to investigate such things as physical changes, the socioeconomic implications of the eruption and the loss of life. Ask them to reflect on what it would have been like to have been present at the various eruptions. **(interpersonal intelligence, higher-order thinking and reasoning)**

- Finally, students individually reflect on their own lives and use volcanic processes as metaphors in telling their life stories or writing about their life experiences (for example, "Eruptions in My Life"). **(intrapersonal intelligence, higher-order thinking and reasoning)**

Tips and Preparation for Presenting the Unit

1. When working with the personal intelligences, remember that by their very nature they must draw on all the other intelligences. Therefore, encourage students to design their museum displays however they wish, using such features as dioramas, three-dimensional sculptures or models, role plays, music or soundtracks, or whatever their creativity inspires.

2. Video footage of recent volcanic eruptions will help drive home some of the effects of volcanic activity on society. It would also be great to find pictures of volcanoes erupting to put up on the walls so students are surrounded by them as they work. You can often get materials by writing to various volcano research and monitoring organizations.

3. Giving students a short example of your personal volcanic life story will give them a model and probably help them come up with their own. Make the story funny and use the language, concepts, and processes studied during the unit to refer to things in your own life experience. A strategy that is often effective is simply to make a two-column chart. In the first column, list the terms and processes, then in the second column, brainstorm experiences from your own life that in some way correspond to each item in the first column.

4. You may have to do a little background research to help students access the necessary information on recent volcanic activity. You don't have to do in-depth research, but it is helpful to be able to point students in the right direction so they don't waste time trying to locate the resources.

Table 18: Cognitive Levels and Personal Intelligences in Volcanoes and Me Lesson

Cognitive Taxonomy Level	Learning Activities for Personal Intelligences
Higher-Order Thinking & Reasoning Students learn about the impact of volcanoes on peoples in different parts of the world and reflect on their own lives using volcanic metaphors and similes. **3**	**Interpersonal:** Students study recent or famous volcanic eruptions and activity around the world and try to empathize with people who experienced a volcano's fury. **Intrapersonal:** Students write or tell a story about themselves as a volcano: When have I been like a volcano? (For example, pressure building inside until I erupted.) How am I like a volcano today? (For example, which parts of my life are still bubbling; which parts are like the different kinds of lava?)
Analyzing & Processing Information Students study the various processes of volcanic activity from the welling up of magma, to eruption, to formation of a volcano, as well as the geological and socioeconomic impacts of volcanoes on different cultures. **2**	**Interpersonal:** Students divide two research topics among members of their group of four to six. Each pair or trio researches a topic related to the geological processes involved in the formation and eruption of a volcano. **Intrapersonal:** Each pair or trio creates a research plan, shares it with their group and the teacher, then revises the plan in light of the feedback given; at the conclusion of the project, they evaluate the effectiveness of their plan.
Gathering & Understanding Basic Knowledge Students learn about volcanoes, where they are in the world, and what geological and socioeconomic effects they have produced. **1**	**Interpersonal:** Working in small groups, students research the different types of volcanoes, volcanic rocks and landforms, and the different countries where volcanoes exist. In small groups, they share personal experiences with volcanoes or volcanic landforms. **Intrapersonal:** In individual learning logs or thinking diaries, students list the things they already know (or think they know) about volcanoes and questions they have about volcanoes. They share with the class what they hope to learn in the unit.

Higher-Order Thinking, © 2004 Zephyr Press, Chicago, IL • 800-232-2187 • www.zephyrpress.com

Got Health?

A Sample High School Health Unit

In this unit, students learn about everything that is involved in living a healthy lifestyle. The unit begins with groups of students reviewing or learning the basic terminology, concepts, and definitions necessary for a meaningful understanding or discussion of health-ful living (for example, what calories are, how to understand nutrition labels on foods, and the relationship between specific amounts of cardiovascular activity and the number of calories burned). In the second phase of the unit, students interview at least three different health professionals in the community to find out what these experts feel are the key factors to maintaining a healthy lifestyle. The last part of the unit asks students to apply what they have learned to society as a whole. The intelligences and levels of the cognitive taxonomy being tapped are inserted in the outline in bold and summarized in table 19 (page 98).

- To begin, have students divide into small groups. Give each group a list of important terminology and concepts to research. Allow each group to determine how they will divide up the terms within the group and how they will present their findings to the class. **(interpersonal intelligence, gathering and understanding basic knowledge)**

- In personal journals students individually reflect on how the concepts they have learned are relevant in their own lives. They informally evaluate which of these factors are present in their lives and which they would like to have more of. **(intrapersonal intelligence, gathering and understanding basic knowledge)**

- Once they have a thorough understanding of the terms and concepts related to healthy living, students create a survey about factors that promote optimal health. Encourage each student to survey at least three health professionals with a range of different perspectives; for example, their own doctor, a fitness trainer at a local health club, an employee at a health food store, or someone knowledgeable about holistic health practices. Students summarize and compile their findings for the rest of the class, then work to create consensus in the class regarding the key factors in good health, based on their interviews. **(interpersonal intelligence, analyzing and processing information)**

- Assign the class to begin keeping a health journal or health diary in which they reflect on the healthfulness of their own lifestyles. As the first entry, ask them to prioritize the factors that the class agreed were important, and to explain why they ranked the factors in that order. Encourage them to log their healthy and unhealthy practices each day for at least a month. **(intrapersonal intelligence, analyzing and processing information)**

- In cooperative groups of three or four, students research and analyze various diets and health programs currently being promoted in the media (for example, the Atkins diet, the Jenny Craig program, infomercials on various vitamin supplements or health remedies, exercise programs touted on television or in local health clubs, or the advice of health gurus such as Andrew Weil). Each group chooses three different programs or approaches to healthy living to research in detail. They evaluate the pros and cons of each, and present their conclusions about the most effective program to the rest of the class in the form of their own infomercials. **(interpersonal intelligence, higher-order thinking and reasoning)**

- Finally, students fully analyze the state of their own health, based on information they have gleaned from the unit. They create a plan for gradually improving the state of their own health over the next several months. Ask students to share with a partner any of these personal reflections they wish to share. **(intrapersonal intelligence, higher-order thinking and reasoning)**

Tips and Preparation for Presenting the Unit

1. When working with the personal intelligences, remember that by their very nature, they must draw on all the other intelligences. Therefore, encourage groups to design their reports however they wish, using such features as dioramas, three-dimensional sculptures or models, role plays, music or soundtracks, or whatever their creativity inspires.

2. Identify and contact people for the students to survey about health practices. Generate a list of people who agree to be interviewed but establish parameters to ensure they are not overwhelmed with calls, such as allowing no more than three interviews of one professional.

3. Do some advance research to select different health programs for students to investigate. Write these on index cards and place them in a hat. Have each group draw three to research. This will save time and help students focus on the research rather than the search for programs to research.

4. To save time, also suggest ways students can research their assigned program (for example, websites to visit, local addresses, and prearranged contacts for them to interview).

5. You may want to arrange for outside assistance in filming the infomercials in the final part of the unit. Such assistance will help students focus on the content of their presentations, rather than being distracted by the technology.

Table 19: Cognitive Levels and Personal Intelligences in Got Health? Lesson

Cognitive Taxonomy Level	Learning Activities for Personal Intelligences
Higher-Order Thinking & Reasoning Students examine popular approaches to healthful living available today and evaluate the relative plusses and minuses of each. Based on their research, they design a personal plan that they feel will lead them to optimal health. **3** ↑	**Interpersonal:** Teams research different health programs available today; they analyze the pros and cons of each, and create an infomercial that reflects the team's consensus on the best program or approach to live a healthy life for presentation to the class. **Intrapersonal:** Students create individual personal health profiles in which they analyze their own lives, noting healthy and unhealthy aspects of their lifestyles. They create strategic plans to increase the healthfulness of their own lives.
Analyzing & Processing Information Students study the factors involved in creating a healthy lifestyle, evaluate the relative importance of each factor, and reflect on how they personally feel about each of the factors that experts claim contribute to optimal health. **2** ↑	**Interpersonal:** Students create a survey on factors in optimal health. Each student interviews health professionals in the community to learn as much as possible from actual practitioners about what contributes to a healthy lifestyle. Students share the results of their surveys with the class and build consensus on the most important factors. **Intrapersonal:** Each student individually ranks the factors the class rated from most to least important to him or her personally. The student then writes a brief journal entry explaining the rationale for the rankings.
Gathering & Understanding Basic Knowledge Students study and learn the vocabulary necessary for understanding healthful living, and they reflect on their own lifestyles using the appropriate vocabulary. **1**	**Interpersonal:** Each small group of students receives a list of terms related to healthy living. They divide the terms among themselves, look up the meanings of the words, and plan how to teach their terms to the rest of the class. **Intrapersonal:** In personal journals, students reflect on how the health concepts are relevant in their own lives and which they would like to develop further.

Higher-Order Thinking, © 2004 Zephyr Press, Chicago, IL • 800-232-2187 • www.zephyrpress.com

Unit Planning Process
Using the Taxonomies_____

Following is a process for using the multiple taxonomies for multiple intelligences to design a unit that moves students' thinking to higher-order realms, both in the content area of the unit and in the intelligences you are using to teach the various concepts of the unit. Feel free to copy the planning worksheet on page 101 as many times as needed to accommodate the concepts in the unit. In fact, you may want to enlarge the sheet to give you more space to write the details of your plan.

1. At the bottom of column 1, write the key curriculum concepts you will be teaching and students will be studying during the unit.

2. Now move up through the different levels of the taxonomy, stating what content the student must master at the gathering and under-standing basic knowledge, information analysis and processing, and higher-order thinking and reasoning levels, respectively. State as clearly as you can what content should be mastered at each level.

3. At the bottom of columns 2, 3, and 4 select three different intelligences around which to plan your unit—one intelligence from the object-related intelligences, one from the object-free intelligences, and one from the personal intelligences. This will ensure a balance of differ-ent cognitive abilities as well as provide for the maximum activation of different areas of the brain. Choose intelligences that you believe are a good match for the content and concepts you'll be teaching.

4. Next, from the taxonomy charts presented in chapters 2 to 4 of the book, select the specific cognitive abilities you will use from the intel-ligences you have chosen. These constitute the range of learning techniques and methods you will use in teaching the unit and those students will use in their learning.

5. Use the taxonomy charts in chapters 2 to 4 to guide you in planning specific activities for each level of the unit. Use the taxonomies to "jump-start" your own creative thought processes. Your goal is to *mesh* the concepts of the unit with the cognitive abilities of the intelligences *in such a way that the intelligences help you move students' thinking to the higher-order realms.*

6. Finally, map out the strategies you have listed on the chart on a time line for teaching the unit. Remember, *your goal is to have students spend as much time as possible at the information analysis and processing and higher-order thinking and reasoning levels of the unit.* In order to do this, they need to complete a certain amount of gathering and understanding of the facts and figures at the first level—just don't overdo this part! Also don't worry about overlap when you're laying out the unit time line. The eight intelligences work together in well-orchestrated ways in almost every task we perform. You will rarely see an intelligence operating in isolation from the others.

Multiple Taxonomies for Multiple Intelligences Unit Planning Worksheet

	1. Curriculum Concepts	2. Object-Related Intelligences	3. Object-Free Intelligences	4. Personal Intelligences
Higher-Order Thinking & Reasoning **3**				
Information Analysis & Processing **2**				
Gathering Basic Knowledge **1**				

Curriculum Concepts	Multiple Intelligences		
• _____ • _____ • _____ • _____ • _____ • _____ • _____ • _____ • _____	**Object-Related Intelligences** _____ _____ _____	**Object-Free Intelligences** _____ _____ _____	**Personal Intelligences** _____ _____ _____

Bibliography ———————————————

Works Cited

Bloom, B., ed. 1956. *Taxonomy of Educational Objectives: The Classification of Educational Goals.* New York: Longmans Green.

Bruner, J. S. 1966. *Toward a Theory of Instruction.* Cambridge, Mass.: Belknap Press.

Buzan, T. 1991. *Use Both Sides of Your Brain: New Mind-Mapping Techniques to Help You Raise All Levels of Your Intelligence and Creativity, Based on the Latest Discoveries about the Human Brain.* New York: Dutton.

Gardner, H. 1983. *Frames of Mind: The Theory of Multiple Intelligences.* New York: Basic Books.

————. 1987. Developing the Spectrum of Human Intelligences: Teaching in the Eighties: A Need to Change. *Harvard Educational Review* 57: 87–93.

————. 1999. *Intelligence Reframed: Multiple Intelligences for the Twenty-First Century.* New York: Basic Books.

Lazear, D. 1998a. *Eight Ways of Knowing: Teaching for Multiple Intelligences.* Arlington Heights, Ill.: Skylight Training and Publishing.

————. 1998b. *The Rubrics Way: Using Multiple Intelligences to Assess Understanding.* Tucson, Ariz.: Zephyr Press.

————. 2000. *The Intelligent Curriculum: Using Multiple Intelligences to Develop Your Students' Full Potential.* Tucson, Ariz.: Zephyr Press.

Piaget, J., and B. Inhelder. 1969. *Psychology of the Child.* Trans. Helen Weaver. New York: Basic Books.

Samuels, M., and N. Samuels. 1975. *Seeing with the Mind's Eye: The History, Techniques, and Uses of Visualization.* New York: Random House.

Wahl, M. 1997. *Math for Humans: Teaching Math through Seven Intelligences.* Langley, Wash.: LivnLern Press.

Further Reading

Armstrong, T. 1987. *In Their Own Way: Discovering and Encouraging Your Child's Personal Learning Style.* Los Angeles: J. P. Tarcher.

—————. 1993. *Seven Kinds of Smart: Identifying and Developing Your Many Intelligences.* New York: Penguin.

Baron, J. 2000. *Thinking and Deciding.* 3rd ed. New York: Cambridge University Press.

Bellanca, J., and R. Fogarty. 1989. *Patterns for Thinking, Patterns for Transfer.* Palatine, Ill.: Skylight.

—————. 2003. *Blueprints for Achievement in the Cooperative Classroom.* 3d. ed. Arlington Heights, Ill.: IRI/Skylight Training and Publishing.

Beyer, B. 1987. *Practical Strategies for the Teaching of Thinking.* Boston: Allyn and Bacon.

Blair, J., and R. N. Caine, eds. 1995. *Integrative Learning as the Pathway to Teaching Holism, Complexity, and Interconnectedness.* Lewiston, N.Y.: Edwin Mellen Press.

Bloom, A. 1987. *The Closing of the American Mind.* New York: Simon and Schuster.

Bolanos, P. J. 1990. Restructuring the Curriculum. *Principal* 69 (3): 13–14.

Brandsford J., A. Brown, and R. Cocking, eds. 1999. *How People Learn: Brain, Mind, Experience, and School.* Washington, D.C.: National Academy Program.

Brophy, J. 1998. *Motivating Students to Learn.* Boston: McGraw-Hill.

Caine, G., R. N. Caine, and S. Crowell. 1999. *MindShifts: A Brain-Compatible Process for Professional Development and the Renewal of Education.* Rev. ed. Tucson, Ariz.: Zephyr Press.

Caine, R. N., and G. Caine. 1990. Understanding a Brain-Based Approach to Learning and Teaching. *Educational Leadership* 48 (2): 66–70.

—————. 1994. *Making Connections: Teaching and the Human Brain.* Rev. ed. Alexandria, Va.: Association for Supervision and Curriculum Development.

—————. 1997. *Education on the Edge of Possibility.* Alexandria, Va.: Association for Supervision and Curriculum Development.

Campbell, B. 1994. *The Multiple Intelligences Handbook: Lesson Plans and More.* Stanwood, Wash.: Stanwood.

Campbell, L., B. Campbell, and D. Dickinson. 1992. *Teaching and Learning through Multiple Intelligences.* Seattle, Wash.: New Horizons for Learning.

Chapman, C. 1993. *If the Shoe Fits . . . How to Develop Multiple Intelligences in the Classroom.* Palatine, Ill.: Skylight.

Clark, E., Jr. 1992. The Search for a New Educational Paradigm. In vol. 1 of *If Minds Matter: A Foreword to the Future*, 25–40. Palatine, Ill.: Skylight.

Costa, A. 1981. Teaching for Intelligent Behavior. *Educational Leadership* 39 (1): 29–31.

————. 1984. Mediating the Metacognitive. *Educational Leadership* 42 (3): 57–62.

————. 1991. *Developing Minds*. Rev. ed. Alexandria, Va.: Association for Supervision and Curriculum Development.

————. 1991. *The School as a Home for the Mind*. Palatine, Ill.: Skylight.

————, ed. 2001. *Developing Minds: A Resource Book for Teaching Thinking*. Alexandria, Va.: Association for Supervision and Curriculum Development.

Costa, A., and B. Kalik, eds. 2000. *Habits of Mind: A Developmental Series*. 2000. Alexandria, Va.: Association for Supervision and Curriculum Development.

Csikszentmihalyi, M. 1991. *Flow: The Psychology of Optimal Experience*. New York: Harper.

Darling-Hammond, L. 1997. *The Right to Learn*. San Francisco: Jossey-Bass.

de Bono, E. 1992. *Serious Creativity: Using the Power of Lateral Thinking to Create New Ideas*. New York: HarperCollins.

Diamond, M. C., and J. Hopson. 1998. *Magic Trees of the Mind: How to Nurture Your Child's Intelligence, Creativity, and Healthy Emotions from Birth through Adolescence*. New York: Dutton.

Dickinson, D. 1987. *New Developments in Cognitive Research*. Seattle, Wash.: New Horizons for Learning.

————. 1992. Technology and the Multiple Intelligences. *Intelligence Connections* 1: 2–3.

————., ed. 1991. *Creating the Future: Perspectives on Educational Change*. Aston Clinton, Bucks., U.K.: Accelerated Learning Systems.

Diez, M. E., and C. J. Moon. 1992. What Do We Want Students to Know? . . . and Other Important Questions. *Educational Leadership* 49 (8): 38–41.

Educational Testing Service and Harvard Project Zero. 1991. *Arts Propel: An Introductory Handbook*. Cambridge, Mass.: Harvard Graduate School of Education.

Eisner, E. 1993. Why Standards May Not Improve Schools. *Educational Leadership* 50 (5): 76–77.

Feuerstein, R. 1980. *Instrumental Enrichment: An Intervention Program for Cognitive Modifiability*. Baltimore, Md.: University Park Press.

Fogarty, R. 1991. *The Mindful School: How to Integrate the Curricula*. Palatine, Ill.: Skylight.

Fulghum, R. 1988. *All I Really Need to Know I Learned in Kindergarten: Uncommon Thoughts on Common Things.* New York: Villard Books.

Gardner. H. 1991. *The Unschooled Mind: How Children Think and How Schools Should Teach.* New York: Basic Books.

————. 1992. *Developmental Psychology: An Introduction.* Boston: Little, Brown.

————. 1993. *Multiple Intelligences: The Theory in Practice.* New York: Basic Books.

————. 1995. Reflections on Multiple Intelligences: Myths and Messages. *Phi Delta Kappan* 77 (3): 200–3, 206–9.

————. 1999. *The Disciplined Mind: What All Students Should Understand.* New York: Simon and Schuster.

Glasser, W. 1986. *Control Theory in the Classroom.* New York: Perennial Library.

Glatthorn, A. A. 1994. *Developing a Quality Curriculum.* Alexandria, Va.: Association for Supervision and Curriculum Development.

Glickman, C. 1991. Pretending Not to Know What We Know. *Educational Leadership* 48 (8): 4–9.

Goleman, D. 1995. *Emotional Intelligence.* New York: Bantam Books.

Gorman, B., and W. Johnson. 1991. *Successful Schooling for Everyone.* Bloomington, Ind.: National Educational Services.

Gould, S. 1981. *The Mismeasure of Man.* New York: Norton.

Gregorc, A. 1982. *A Style Delineator.* Maynard, Mass.: Gabriel Systems.

Guilford, J. P. 1967. *The Nature of Human Intelligence.* New York: McGraw-Hill.

Haggerty, B. 1995. *Nurturing Intelligences: A Guide to Multiple Intelligence Theory and Practice.* New York: Addison Wesley.

Hansen, J. M., and J. Childs. 1998. Creating a School Where People Like to Be. *Educational Leadership* 56 (1): 14–17.

Harman, W. 1988. *The Global Mind Change: The Promise of the Last Years of the Twentieth Century.* Indianapolis, Ind.: Knowledge Systems.

Harman, W., and H. Rheingold. 1985. *Higher Creativity: Liberating the Unconscious for Breakthrough Insights.* Los Angeles: J. P. Tarcher.

Harris, P. 1992. Restructuring for Learning. In vol. 1 of *If Minds Matter: A Foreword to the Future.* Palatine, Ill.: Skylight.

Hart, L. 1983. *Human Brain and Human Learning.* Village of Oak Creek, Ariz.: Books for Educators.

Hoerr, T. 2000. *Becoming an MI School: Using Multiple Intelligences for Student and*

Teacher Success. Alexandria, Va.: Association for Supervision and Curriculum Development.

Houston, J. 1980. *Lifeforce: The Psycho-Historical Recovery of the Self.* New York: Delacorte Press.

————. 1982. *The Possible Human: A Course in Extending Your Physical, Mental, and Creative Abilities.* Los Angeles: J. P. Tarcher.

Isaacs, W. 1999. *Dialogue and the Art of Thinking Together.* New York: Currency.

Isaksen, S. G., B. Dorval, and D. J. Treffinger. 2000. *Creative Approaches to Problem Solving: A Framework for Change.* Dubuque, Iowa: Kendall/Hunt.

Jacobs, H. H. 1990. *Interdisciplinary Curriculum: Design and Implementation.* Alexandria, Va.: Association for Supervision and Curriculum Development.

Jacobs, H. H., and J. H. Borland. 1986. The Interdisciplinary Concept Model: Theory and Practice. *Gifted Child Quarterly* 30 (4): 159–63.

Jensen, E. 1998. *Teaching with the Brain in Mind.* Alexandria, Va.: Association for Supervision and Curriculum Development.

Kagan, S., and M. Kagan. 1998. *Multiple Intelligences: The Complete MI Book.* San Clemente, Calif.: Kagan Cooperative Learning.

Kalick, B. 1989. *Changing Schools into Communities for Thinking.* Grand Forks: N.D.: University of North Dakota Press.

Kohn, A. 1996. *Beyond Discipline: From Compliance to Community.* Alexandria, Va.: Association for Supervision and Curriculum Development.

Kovalik, S. 1993. *Integrated Thematic Instruction: The Model.* Village of Oak Creek, Ariz.: Susan Kovalik and Associates.

Krechevsky, M. 1991. Project Spectrum: An Innovative Assessment Alternative. *Educational Leadership* 48 (5): 43–48.

Krechevsky, M., T. Hoerr, and H. Gardner. 1995. Complementary Energies: Implementing MI Theory from the Lab and from the Field. In *Creating New Educational Communities: Schools and Classrooms Where All Children Can Be Smart.* Ed. Jeannie Oakes and Karen H. Quartz, 166–86. Chicago: University of Chicago Press.

Lazear, D. 1989. Multiple Intelligences and How We Nurture Them. *Cogitore* 4 (1): 1, 4–5.

————. 1998. *Eight Ways of Teaching: The Artistry of Teaching with Multiple Intelligences.* Arlington Heights, Ill.: Skylight.

————. 1998. *Multiple Intelligence Approaches to Assessment: Solving the Assessment Conundrum.* Rev. ed. Tucson, Ariz.: Zephyr Press.

———. 1999. *Pathways of Learning: Teaching Students and Parents about Multiple Intelligences.* Tucson, Ariz.: Zephyr Press.

McTighe, J., and G. Wiggins. 1999. *Understanding by Design Handbook.* Alexandria, Va.: Association for Supervision and Curriculum Development.

National Science Foundation. 2000. Inquiry: Thoughts, Views, and Strategies for K–5 Classrooms. In Vol. 2 of *Foundations.* Arlington, Va.: National Academy Press.

New City School Faculty. 1994. *Celebrating Multiple Intelligences: Teaching for Success.* St. Louis, Mo.: New City School.

———. 1996. *Succeeding with Multiple Intelligences: Teaching through the Personal Intelligences.* St. Louis, Mo.: New City School.

Orlich, D. 1994. *Teaching Strategies.* Lexington, Mass.: D. C. Heath.

Paul, R., and L. Elder. 2001. *Critical Thinking: Tools for Taking Charge of Your Learning and Your Life.* New York: Prentice Hall.

Perkins, D. 1992. *Smart Schools: From Training Memories to Educating Minds.* New York: Free Press.

———. 1995. *Outsmarting IQ: The Emerging Science of Learnable Intelligence.* New York: Free Press.

Perkins, D., and G. Solomon. 1988. Teaching for Transfer. *Educational Leadership* 46 (1): 22–32.

Piaget, J. 1972. *The Psychology of Intelligence.* Totowa, N. J.: Littlefield Adams.

Resnick, L. B., and L. Klopfer. 1989. *Toward the Thinking Curriculum: Current Cognitive Research.* Alexandria, Va.: Association for Supervision and Curriculum Development.

Rourke, J. 2001. Why Is Mona Lisa Smiling? *Principal Leadership* 2 (3). Available from http://www.principals.org/news/pl_monalisa1101.cfm

Rubado, K. 2002. Empowering Students through Multiple Intelligences. *Reclaiming Children and Youth* 10 (4): 233–35.

Russell, P. 1995. *The Global Brain Awakens: Our Next Evolutionary Leap.* Palo Alto, Calif.: Global Brain.

Schlechty, P. 1990. *Schools for the Twenty-First Century.* San Francisco: Jossey-Bass.

Sizer, T. R., and B. Rogers. 1993. Designing Standards: Achieving the Delicate Balance. *Educational Leadership* 50 (5): 24–26.

Smith, F. 1986. *Insult to Intelligences: The Bureaucratic Invasion of Our Classrooms.* Portsmouth, N.H.: Heinemann Educational.

Sternberg, R. 1984. *Beyond I.Q.: A Triarchic Theory of Human Intelligence.* New York: Cambridge University Press.

————. 1984. How Can We Teach Intelligence? *Educational Leadership* 42 (1): 38–48.

————. 1986. *Intelligence Applied: Understanding and Increasing Your Intellectual Skills.* San Diego: Harcourt Brace Jovanovich.

————. 1991. Thinking Styles: Keys to Understanding Student Performance. *Inquiry: Critical Thinking across the Disciplines* 7 (3): 32–38.

Stiggins, R., E. Rubel, and E. Quellmalz. 1986. *Measuring Thinking Skills in the Classroom: A Teacher's Guide.* Portland, Ore.: Northwest Regional Laboratory.

Sylwester, R. 2003. *A Biological Brain in a Cultural Classroom: Enhancing Cognitive and Social Development through Collaborative Classroom Management.* 2d ed. Thousand Oaks, Calif.: Corwin Press.

Teele, S. 2000. *Rainbows of Intelligence: Exploring How Students Learn.* Thousand Oaks, Calif.: Corwin Press.

Ulrey, D., and J. Ulrey. 1992. Developmentally Appropriate Practices Meet Multiple Intelligences. *Intelligence Connections* 2 (1): 4–6.

Wagmeister, J., and B. Shifrin. 2000. Thinking Differently, Learning Differently. *Educational Leadership* 58 (3): 45–48.

Wiggins, G. 1991. Standards, Not Standardization: Evoking Quality Student Work. *Educational Leadership* 58 (3): 45–48.

Wolfe, P. 2001. *Brain Matters: Translating Research into Classroom Practice.* Alexandria, Va.: Association for Supervision and Curriculum Development.

Index

About the Author

David Lazear is the founder of New Dimensions of Learning, an organization that trains educators and businesspeople to apply cutting-edge research on multiple intelligences and other brain-friendly approaches to instruction. He has had many years of international experience in practical applications of multiple intelligences theory to classroom, school, and business settings. David is the author of several products about the practical

implementation of MI theory, including *The Intelligent Curriculum: Using Multiple Intelligences to Develop Your Students' Full Potential, Pathways of Learning: Teaching Students and Parents about Multiple Intelligences, Multiple Intelligence Approaches to Assessment: Solving the Assessment Conundrum, The Rubrics Way: Using Multiple Intelligences to Assess Understanding,* and *Tap Your Multiple Intelligences* posters, co-developed with Nancy Margulies. His latest book for the popular market is *OutSmart Yourself! 16 Proven Strategies for Becoming Smarter Than You Think You Are.*

M1067774 12.09:07
048656 371.30281 LAT
£19.99.   TV

M1067774 12.09:07
048656 371.30281 LAT
£19.99.